SPOTLIGHT ON CRITICAL SKILLS IN ESSAY WRITING

CAROLE ANNE MAY

Camosun College

PEARSON

Prentice
Hall

Toronto

Library and Archives Canada Cataloguing in Publication

May, Carole Anne, 1948–
    Spotlight on critical skills in essay writing / Carole Anne May.

Includes index.
ISBN 0-13-114390-5

    1. English language—Rhetoric. 2. Essay—Authorship. 3. Report writing. I. Title.

PE1471.M39 2007   808'.042   C2006-900972-4

ISBN 0-13-114390-5

Vice President, Editorial Director: Michael J. Young
Acquisitions Editor: Patty Riediger
Marketing Manager: Leigh-Anne Graham
Signing Representative: Carmen Batsford
Developmental Editor: Matthew Christian
Production Editor: Richard di Santo
Copy Editor: Linda Cahill
Proofreader: Nancy Carroll
Production Coordinator: Janis Raisen
Permissions Manager: Susan Wallace-Cox
Permissions Research: Lynn McIntyre
Composition: Janet Zanette
Art Director: Julia Hall
Cover and Interior Design: Gillian Tsintziras
Cover Image: Nonstock

1 2 3 4 5   11 10 09 08 07

Printed and bound in the United States of America.

dedication

This book is dedicated to my brother, Ron, and to my sister-in-law, Cindy.
Thank you for your love, friendship, and support over the years.

brief contents

detailed contents

preface

Spotlight on Critical Skills in Essay Writing is designed for first-year or college preparation students who must develop their writing skills in order to succeed in future college or university courses. As students work thoughtfully through the text, they will progress through skill-building that culminates in the gains of broader-based composition expertise. In the foreground is the development of critical thinking, reading, and writing skills, while in the background is the text's clear sequence that builds application with varied exercises—both individual and collaborative—from the prewriting phases, to college essay writing, to research paper writing. This textbook contains challenging chapters and exercises for practice and application of foundational concepts in grammar and mechanics. Special Bonus Exercises at the end of most chapters give students the opportunity to learn about common errors they make in their writing, and offer exercises to improve their editing skills and eliminate these common errors.

Spotlight on Critical Skills in Essay Writing includes elements most instructors want to see in a textbook. The critical thinking skills of summarizing, paraphrasing, comparing and contrasting, evaluating, analyzing, persuading, researching, and synthesizing information are taught directly through chapter work. Rhetorical patterns are developed throughout writing chapters and in an extensive readings chapter. Collaborative work is encouraged through a variety of exercises. Extensive explanations and examples are provided throughout the text. Editing and style notes are carefully explained in a special chapter. Developing a vocabulary for college is also discussed in a separate chapter. Reading comprehension questions accompany each reading in the readings chapter. Self-tests and review tests offer students practice in developing key skills for planning, composing, writing, researching, and editing.

Spotlight on Critical Skills in Essay Writing offers clear and extensive explanations of many aspects of English study. For example, students learn format and structure from rhetorical modes, but they also learn to observe how writers express themselves and to shape their own writing efforts; as a result, while students become better at expressing themselves more concisely, they also become familiar with academic discourse. In addition, they learn the planning strategies that are crucial for developmental writers. Students require the opportunity to develop their written language capabilities through the interplay of thinking and writing. Moreover, academically-bound students require critical skill proficiencies in order to succeed in academic contexts. In recognition of this, *Spotlight on Critical Skills in Essay Writing* is intended to be a textbook from which students can learn what they need to know. Its goal is to develop students' belief in their own potential and academic success because positive educational experiences will transform their lives.

Key Features

Spotlight on Critical Skills in Essay Writing has many useful and important features:

- Two chapters (Chapters 1 and 2) deal with **pre-writing** and **planning strategies** for writing.

- A complete chapter on **narrative writing** (Chapter 5) will help students to reflect on the richness and power of their own experience as a transformative tool. The chapter includes special narrative readings and exercises.

- A full chapter covers **expository** writing and **five rhetorical modes** (Chapter 6).

- A special chapter deals with **summarizing and paraphrasing strategies** and exercises (Chapter 7).

- A complete chapter discusses the essential critical-thinking skill of **evaluating** and provides writing exercises based on this skill (Chapter 8).

- Two full chapters cover the art of **persuasion**, including analyzing persuasive techniques and applying them in structuring persuasive pieces (Chapters 9 and 10).

- Three full chapters explain **research writing**, including a chapter that introduces the research paper (Chapter 11), another that discusses and offers practice in APA and MLA styles (Chapter 12), and a third that discusses the writing of a research paper (Chapter 13). Particular attention is paid to plagiarism and the use of online sources.

- An extensive chapter on **editing and style notes** (Chapter 14) includes editing tips for eliminating common errors in punctuation and grammar. It also contains style notes on special items like the active and the passive voice, logical constructions, sentence variety, and cohesive devices.

- A special and comprehensive chapter develops **college vocabulary** (Chapter 15).

- The unique readings chapter (Chapter 16) offers **reading comprehension** practice while it provides a rich variety of reading selections arranged by rhetorical modes. Seven different types of reading comprehension questions accompany each reading. Each comprehension type develops a particular aspect of reading comprehension: literal comprehension, vocabulary in context, restructuring, inference, prediction, evaluation, and personal response.

- **Bonus Exercises** at the end of each chapter help students develop editing skills through examining common writing errors and offering exercises to help eliminate them.

- Intense and varied opportunities offer students **practice**. Ideas are not merely introduced. Students work through practices designed to develop critical thinking via a series of steps and strategies that encourage engagement and reflection. The structure of the exercises encourages collaborative work among students.

- Exercises are keyed to an **Answer Key** found at the end of the text. The reviews in the grammar chapters do *not* have answer keys so that instructors may choose to use these reviews as chapter tests. The review answer keys are available in the Instructor's Manual that accompanies the text.

- Both **self-tests** and **review tests** are offered for most chapters. These learning tools have proved to be effective for students entering college or university.

- The approach and instructional content have been **field-tested** over a number of years with college students. Overall, students reported enjoyment of the approach and the nature of the exercises and assignments, as well as satisfaction with the improvement in their abilities to think critically, analyze, organize, and construct written material.

- Through its philosophy and structure, the book **encourages students to become capable and confident**, and ready to handle higher-level challenges in their writing. It emphasizes the concept of writing as a complex process, as a recursive undertaking, and as an individual project that has phases.

Faculty Supplements

Spotlight on Critical Skills in Essay Writing is accompanied by an Instructor's Manual that is an invaluable resource for anyone using this textbook. Included in the Instructor's Manual are review test answers, suggested activities, and additional answers for exercises found in the text. This supplement can be downloaded by instructors from a password-protected location on Pearson Education Canada's online catalogue (vig.pearsoned.ca). Simply search for the text, then click on "Instructor" under "Resources" in the left-hand menu. Contact your local sales representative for further information.

Acknowledgments

Thanks are due to the many reviewers whose feedback on the original proposal or manuscript chapters has helped to shape the project, including the following people:

   Heather Gosein, Georgian College
   Nancy Holmes, Okanagan University College
   Peter C. Miller, Seneca College of Applied Arts and Technology
   Kathleen Moran, Conestoga College
   Nina Pyne, Sault College
   Melanie A. Rubens, Seneca College of Applied Arts and Technology

I am especially grateful to Pearson Education Canada for the opportunity to bring this series of books forward. Patty Riediger (Acquisitions Editor), Matthew Christian (Senior Developmental Editor), Richard di Santo (Production Editor), Linda Cahill (Copy Editor), and Nancy Carroll (Proofreader) have been outstanding in their encouragement and expert support.

chapter 1

Writing as Process: Prewriting

Chapter Objectives

What will you have learned when you have completed this chapter?
You will be able to

1. recognize phases of writing.

2. develop ways to deal with procrastination.

3. pique interest in your writing.

4. generate writing ideas.

5. determine your purpose in writing.

6. choose a suitable writing tone.

Introduction

Writing is the development of ideas, the expression of thoughts using words, and a set of practices. As such, writing is a process because it involves a series of inter-related steps, producing changes that result in some sort of written outcome—a review, an essay, a journal, a research paper, or something else like a poem, a short story, a play, a film script, or a novel. Almost all students engage in some kind of writing activity in the course of their studies, and almost all learn and improve.

As a writer, you must recognize that writing is a process: You write, revise, edit, rework, and often rethink a piece of writing. The process is not like taking a bus from point A and arriving in a more or less straight line to point B. Although writing, like bus travel, has many stops along the way, it can move in different directions: backwards, sideways, in circles, randomly, and so on. Unlike the bus, you cannot predict with accuracy exactly which direction the writing will take you. If bus travel were like writing, some passengers might find themselves ending up in strange and surprising destinations.

It is quite fine and normal to find the writing process a little bit messy. You may have to rework the introduction of a paper after you have adjusted other parts. With some trepidation, you may discover an outline needs reworking or a great idea that came to you at three in the morning looks pretty weak in the hard, cold light of noon. Recognize that unexpected turns are part of the bumpy journey in writing. *Spotlight on Critical Skills in Essay and Research Writing* offers the writing process as six phases: Chapter 1 presents phase 1, prewriting, while Chapter 2 discusses phases 2–6, planning, drafting, revising, editing, and presenting.

Self-Test

Try the following self-test. It will help you assess your knowledge of the writing process and your own writing habits. There are no strictly "correct" or "incorrect" answers. Be prepared to share your responses with others in the class.

Part 1: Name three techniques you use to prepare for writing.

1. _____
2. _____
3. _____

Part 2: As a writer, how do you get your ideas?

_____

_____

_____

Part 3: Name three purposes for writing.

1. _____
2. _____
3. _____

Part 4: What is point of view in writing?

_____

_____

_____

Part 5: What is tone in writing?

_____

_____

_____

Part 6: What is procrastination? Do you ever do it? Why?

_____

_____

_____

*Part 7: What techniques do you have for defeating procrastination?
Name two.*

1. _____

2. _____

Overview: Phases of Writing

Writing does not always "happen" in the same way, but writing does usually occur as a process that includes several phases. As a writer, you think about what you are going to write: you might make idea notes, you might discuss your ideas with friends, and you might do some research on your topic. You might be doing more than one thing at a time when it comes to your preparation for writing; it all depends on what the situation is, how much time you have, how much time you are willing to commit, and what your purpose in writing is.

The phases of writing are not clear-cut, but experts do agree that most writers experience most or all of them at different times. Each writing experience you have will be unique—an interesting combination of what you have learned and what you choose to apply to the task at hand. Clearly, more complex writing tasks, like research papers, will require more preparation while simpler or shorter tasks will require less.

The following sections introduce you to the phases of writing. Remember that you may not use all of the phases in all writing situations; however, you should be utilizing the important phases in most writing situations.

Phase 1: Prewriting

Prewriting refers to the preparatory work you put in before you begin to write a draft. Prewriting is a stage wherein you think and prepare to write. It may include reading and taking notes, sketching ideas, outlining, and discussion, but it may include other activities that help generate ideas and inspiration.

To Procrastinate or Not

One of the most important parts of the writing process comes at the start. Have you noticed how difficult it seems to get something started at times? You can think of examples from your own life. Perhaps, for instance, you have work to do around your home, yet you find yourself putting it off in order to do something else, usually of lesser importance. Do you find yourself doing the laundry when what you really need to do is get started on a research paper? Do you find yourself watching a silly television program instead of doing the reading for your English literature class? You might say, "yes" to a group of friends who want you to go out with them when you really ought to say, "no." Almost all students will report similar experiences, and they will also talk about the guilt they feel at not making the best choices for time management. That's the starting point: to recognize that procrastination, the putting off of a task or assignment, is a normal response, maybe even a useful one. Like everyone else, you need to learn strategies to deal with it.

Procrastination is the result of a number of issues, but rarely laziness. It might mean you feel uncertain. Maybe the challenge seems too great. Maybe you feel shy about asking your instructor to help clarify an assignment. Perhaps previously you have had negative experiences with a subject like English and feel anxious about it. Examine your feelings: Do you put off doing an assignment for any of these reasons?

It is true that frequently students put off course-related things, not necessarily because they are bad planners or people, but rather because they are really not sure what they are supposed to do in an assignment. If this is the case for you, then try these strategies:

1. Find someone else in the class who looks organized. Ask this student if he or she would mind talking with you briefly after class because you want to make sure you have understood each assignment correctly. Tell your new colleague that you often misunderstand assignments and need help with clarification.
2. Contact your instructor. Email is an excellent tool. In your email, tell your instructor that you need help with clarification. Don't write a long-winded message, full of excuses and apologies. Be polite, direct, and concise. Most instructors will respond quickly to your request. If an assignment is complex, use email to book an appointment with your instructor, or visit him or her during posted office hours.

If you procrastinate because you feel anxious due to some previous history with the subject, you can develop coping strategies.

1. Look for another student in your course or program who you think is a good listener, well-organized, trustworthy, and friendly. Ask to meet for coffee and tell the student why you want to talk to him or her. When you meet, be fairly straightforward about your experiences, but try to be specific. You might say something like this: "When I was in high school, I didn't do well in English. Now that I think about it, I'm not really sure why. I do know I had a habit of putting things off until the last minute. Then I would hand in whatever trash I had written. Soon I formed a habit of doing this, and my teachers started getting the impression that I was lazy or incompetent. I didn't like that feeling much. Now I have a chance to start again, but I'm not sure how. Have you ever experienced the same situation? What did you do about it?"
2. Every college and university campus has a Learning Help Centre and special resource counsellors who can help you. If you are not comfortable talking with another student, then consider getting some advice from an on-campus expert.

Whatever you do, don't get stuck. Putting something off for a short time may actually allow you to develop some "thinking space." Cognitive psychology now suggests that thinking takes many forms—what you believe to be procrastination may be something else: working something through, a kind of mental mulling over. Here are some other tips that might help you:

1. Recognize when you are procrastinating. Think about your reasons: Are you feeling anxious? Are you unclear about the assignment? Have you made some poor choices about what to do with your time?

2. Set a deadline and immediately start taking action. Procrastination ends when you take action. Do something right away. You can read for 10 minutes. You can work on an Internet search. You can write in your journal. You can read your text and take notes. You can pack up and head off to the library. You can read on the bus on the way to work. You can always take action of some sort, no matter how small it might seem. The old saying, "A journey of a thousand miles begins with a single step" is certainly true.

3. Set small goals. Write them in your day timer or journal. Make the goals achievable. Don't promise yourself something you cannot deliver. In other words, make your first step a reasonable one. For example, you might say, "This evening I plan to reread what my assignment is and to brainstorm for ideas for 30 minutes."

4. When you begin to feel bogged down, talk with someone. The person does not have to be in the same course as you. He or she can be a friend or family member who is a willing and sympathetic listener. Conversation can help in so many ways: It can generate ideas or clarify them. It can lift your spirits. It can help you take action.

5. Use a journal to express and discuss your delay. Take a fresh sheet in your journal and write—without stopping—for 10 minutes. Write about anything connected to your procrastination and your assignment. Write without pausing. Write without stopping to think out what you have to say. Start with this sentence, "I think I know why I am procrastinating over my term paper. . . ." After 10 minutes (set a timer), read over what you have written.

Now you are ready to work. Start with phase 1, prewriting. Prewriting is a preparatory step to writing. It is an activity or set of activities to help focus your attention, ideas, and writing. In Chapter 2, you will read about the rest of the phases. After you have worked through some activities to get you started, you can assess what you have, sort through it, and then set up a plan for writing.

Interest

Interest is a motivator. When you write, think of interest in two ways. Think of you—what interests you and what gets you interested in writing—and your reader, how your writing might interest him or her. Obvious as it may seem, the more interested you are in a topic or assignment, the better the paper you will produce. Chances are if you are not interested in the topic or the writing, you will produce a rather dull paper. Both you and your reader will be sorely disappointed with the result. Interest, then, is something to think about.

How do writers pique their own interest? How do they get started? What sorts of tricks do they have?

Developing Your Interest

First of all, consider what interest might mean to you. Interesting topics can lead to interesting papers. Ask yourself some questions:

- What sorts of topics do I find myself reading about?
- Do I really want to know about something?

- Are there topics I want to explore that are related to a future career path?
- What do I usually do to pursue a topic I am interested in?
- Where do I go to look for new, interesting ideas?

For a writer, a good tool to use is an ideas book. An ideas book is exactly what it sounds like: It is a book you carry with you in which you write down ideas you have throughout the day. Perhaps they are story ideas if you are considering taking a creative writing course. Maybe they are ideas for research. Possibly you have ideas about books, stories, or articles you want to read, or authors you wish to research. You might list literary criticism and comment, and topic ideas for papers.

The effectiveness of the ideas book comes from using one on a regular basis. For the ideas book to be effective for you, you must have it with you, and you must make entries by habit. Journals, for instance, have become very popular with students. Many write in their journals on a daily basis. Journal writing can be extremely beneficial to you if you happen to be one of those people who consistently develop this habit.

An ideas book is somewhat different from a journal. It is really a kind of repository, a place for you to collect and record specific ideas for specific study and research work as the ideas occur to you. While a journal is a place to discuss feelings and events, your ideas book is a gathering place for inspired thoughts, ideas, and study directions.

The ideas book need not be difficult to use or expensive to purchase. You can find three-hole notebooks for less than $2.00 at the dollar store. However, different writers have different preferences. You might favour a smaller, palm-sized memo book since it is an item you can easily tuck into your packsack, purse, or pocket.

Tips for an Ideas Book

- Date each entry.
- Make brief notes.
- Develop your own shorthand for these brief notes. For example, you could make up your own code. "NG" for "not good," "EX" for "excellent" or "example," and so on.
- Keep the book with you wherever you go. Warn your family and friends that you might have to stop to make a quick note from time to time.
- Do not tear out any pages. Sometimes a mediocre idea can lead to more engaging ones.
- Review your ideas book from time to time. Create some plans based on an idea from your book. In other words, if you are about to make a trip to the library, you might check out your ideas book to consolidate some of your research.

Asking Questions for the Ideas Book

Do you recall these questions?

1. What sorts of topics do I find myself reading about?
2. Do I really want to know about something?

3. Are there topics I want to explore that are related to a future career path?
4. What do I usually do to pursue a topic I am interested in?
5. Where do I go to look for new, interesting ideas?

Use these questions after you have purchased your ideas book. Look at the first question. Take a few minutes to answer it. Make a list of topics of interest to you. Write down all ideas—do not censor yourself. Write down the current date and list as many topics of real interest to you as possible. In about one week's time, do the same thing again. Compare the two lists: Are they different? Have you expanded your areas of interest a little since the first entry?

Question 2 asks you what you really want to know about. In your ideas book, write down as many items as you can think of. Your list can contain a wide diversity of queries. For example, you might want to read about a famous sports personality you admire. You might want to know something about his or her life. On the other hand, you might want to know how to organize a conference, train a dog, service a piece of machinery, or practise making a speech. All of these items are arranged according to knowledge of "how to" do something. Similarly, you might want to consider questions relating to abstract ideas, conceptions, or theories. For example, you might want to know what a famous philosopher thought about social conventions such as marriage, what an artist's views on the viewer are, what constitutes a human freedom, or what a feminist might say about *Hamlet*. Write down such questions as they occur to you, but keep them brief and clear.

Review what you really want to know every two weeks. As you revisit your lists, you might suddenly decide to expand one of these questions into a term paper or research essay. You might find some excellent ideas buried in amongst the questions.

Question 3 links to question 2. As you explore what you really want to know about, questions relating to your future career goal may emerge. For example, you may find that the most interesting questions connect to art, art theory, or art criticism if you are a visual arts student.

When you explore your answer to question 4 in your ideas book, you will actually be examining what procedures you use when you investigate something. The question will help you focus on what process you follow, what techniques you use, or what method you develop. Think about what you usually do. Think about what steps you take. Write them down. Then consider whether this process has been effective for you. If you want to improve it, write down some questions you need to answer to improve your research techniques.

Consider this example: Someone assigns a task for you to do; perhaps it is your supervisor, an instructor, or a friend needing help. How do you go about solving the intellectual problem? Do you look for answers on the Internet? Do you talk to someone you trust? Do you look up possible references at the library? Do you take notes? Do you ask an expert? All of these possibilities are valid, but some are more useful than others.

Prior knowledge is important. To select an effective method, you must have some knowledge to begin with. For instance, some tasks require a particular line of inquiry that is more thorough and scholarly. To do a general search on the Internet requires that you know about the process of making an inquiry using a browser and search engine. However, as an academic student you must also know about the scholarly research available online and about how to access it through huge academic databases accessible only through your college or university library site.

To answer question 5 requires an active search. You can find many new and exciting ideas in the professional journals of your academic library on campus. You can note new topics or areas of interest emerging from newscasts, newspaper articles, Internet news, reputable magazines, and television and radio programming. The seminar and discussion groups in your courses will also become important sources for the exchange of ideas and opinions. Even having coffee with a group of your friends from class can be exciting and entertaining if the discussion revolves around ideas. For example, you might want to form a group of interested people from your class who want to meet to discuss two or three important social issues, debate points in articles or materials given out in class, or organize collaborative projects. Go to bookstores, too. You'll see new book releases on current issues or find sections in the store you may not have investigated before. Your campus bookstore may be the place to start. Large universities have excellent campus bookstores with particularly interesting reference sections. In all cases, take advantage of the opportunity to participate, investigate, and learn.

Considering Your Reader's Interest

After you have given some thought to your own interest in the topic and writing about it, you are ready to consider your reader's interest. As you might imagine, it is not always easy to tell exactly what interests your reader or whether what you have to say will interest him or her. However, it is important to consider what factors may be important. This section discusses your audience—the reader—and in that discussion, you will think about which aspects of your reader are most critical to you as the writer.

Your audience is your reader or group of readers. Of course, in some college or university courses, your instructor or professor will be your most important audience because that is who will be evaluating your work. In addition, in many cases, he or she may be the sole reader of your work. However, this scenario is changing. Many courses now include other audiences for students' writing.

1. Collaborative projects demand that you work together with three to five other members of your class to produce one written product. In such a situation, you will find sharing your own writing an important feature of the group project. Some students find it rather odd to share their writing with anyone other than their instructors. In short order, however, they find they must write publicly as part of many courses.

2. Peer-reviewed projects are assignments based on evaluations completed by fellow students of written work done in the class. Some students have not experienced peer reviews before. You, too, might find it somewhat difficult to have another class member review, comment on, and grade your work, yet peer-reviewed assignments are a common practice in most colleges and universities today.

3. Public assignments may include letters to editors, articles written for a class magazine, articles for electronic journals and magazines, or assignments posted for online course work. For example, some instructors ask students to write letters to the editor as part of their course work. Students must then read and respond to comments others may make about their letters. In other circumstances, you may be asked to contribute by writing a short article for a magazine your class assembles. In another situation, if you are taking an online course, you may discover that you must post one of your assignments to your classmates and visitors. Posting means you must put your work in a special section of the course site online where others may read it and make comments about it.

An audience may also be someone you imagine. For example, you might be writing an essay about the life your grandparents have experienced compared to yours. As you write, you might imagine your grandparents reading the piece. You might think of how they would react, what they would say about your work, or what they would want you to explain in your piece. In so doing, you begin to revise your work according to what your imagined (and intended) audience might have to say. Your writing begins to be shaped, then, not only by the topic but also by the intended audience, either real or imagined.

As you write, visualize your reader, imagined or otherwise. If your audience is a "real" one like colleagues, class members, instructors, or professors, you write with a more informed perspective of your reader. You know, more or less, what to expect. You really do know your audience because you have met them. If, on the other hand, you are writing with an imagined audience in mind, you will have to construct some sort of profile of your reader as you write:

- What does your intended reader know about the topic? Are you writing for an expert or an amateur?
- What level of interest do you expect your reader to have? Do you expect your reader to be deeply engaged by the topic or merely have a passing interest in it?
- What do you think is most important in regard to audience and audience interest when you write?

Exercise 1:   Thinking about Audience

Form a group of three to five members. Answer the following questions. Be prepared to share your answers with the class.

1. You are writing a short paper for an online class. What considerations would you make for an audience?

2. You are writing a letter to the editor for an assignment. What considerations would you need to make for your audience? What other considerations might this assignment entail in terms of audience?

3. You are writing an essay for a course in criminology. As part of the course, your instructor asks you to share your paper with a group of social service sector workers. What considerations should you give to your paper in regard to audience and audience interest?

4. You are being asked to write an essay about relationships in families. No specific audience is being named. What would you do in regard to imagining your audience and your audience's interest?

Purpose

Your purpose in writing provides focus. Purposes vary from writer to writer, or from discipline to discipline. However, every writer should understand why he or she is writing something, beyond getting marks for a course.

Before you read more about purpose in this section, try the following exercise.

Exercise 2:   *Thinking about Purpose*

Write down a purpose for each of the following writing scenarios. Think of purpose as the reason or reasons you are writing. Be prepared to share your answers.

1. You have been asked to write a letter to the editor about the crowding on the city buses that take you to college or university each day.

   _____

   _____

2. You have been asked to write a piece about coaching hockey.

   _____

   _____

3. You have been asked to write a piece about poverty and the elderly.

   _____

   _____

4. You have been asked to contribute three pages to a collaborative writing assignment on women in the workplace. Your section of the report is to cover pay equity.

   _____

   _____

5. Your assignment is to describe the typical adult learner. The assignment is for the Continuing Education Department of your college or university. The piece will be posted on their website.

   _____

   _____

Writing can serve different purposes, audiences, and interests. You can think of writing as having four basic purposes:

- to describe
- to narrate (tell a story)
- to convince
- to explain, evaluate, or investigate

Exercise 3:   *Purposes in Writing*

Write down which purpose or purposes each of the following assignments might have. Check your answers with the Answer Key. Be prepared to explain your answers.

1. The assignment is about environment and clear-cutting practices. The purpose or purposes: _____

   _____

2. The assignment is about grading practices in schools. The purpose or purposes:

   _____

   _____

3. The writing assignment is to interview a person living on the streets and then write, using the interview as material for the piece. The purpose or purposes:

   _____

   _____

4. The writing assignment is to compare two writers' use of metaphor in their fiction. The purpose or purposes: _____

   _____

5. The writing assignment is about amateur soccer in Canada. The purpose or purposes:

   _____

   _____

Tone

Tone in writing has to do with your attitude towards your subject or your readers. A writer's tone may be formal or informal, optimistic or pessimistic, serious or comical, angry or joyful, bitter or hopeful; in fact, any emotion or mode of expression may provide the tone.

An ironic tone and a satirical tone need to be mentioned separately because these two expressions describe special circumstances, not emotions. An irony is the opposite of what you expect from a situation or an action: It often expresses something sarcastically or humorously. For example, the statement, "Kim and Bo lost the set of plans they had worked on for eight months" is ironic. What is the irony in the situation?

Satire is a form of ridicule; the writer wants to expose the foolishness or immoral conduct of an individual, group, corporation, or government. Often satire targets some aspect of society, or some "class" in society. Sometimes satires are referred to as "spoofs." Some examples are the Austin Powers movies which spoof the spy films of the 1960s, and political cartoons which satirize political life, heads of state, and government policies and mistakes.

You will find plenty of examples of irony and satire in writing, but life itself has many examples, too. Read the newspaper and look for examples of irony and satire. You might be surprised at what you find.

The tone is also created by the way you say something, including word choice and connotation of the words chosen (positive, negative, or neutral). For example, if you want your tone in writing about gay marriage to be positive, the words you choose should be upbeat and encouraging. The words would support your attitude.

Examples:

Some <u>naive</u> governments tend to <u>meddle</u> in the domestic affairs of other <u>foreign</u> countries. (What is the writer's tone? What is the writer's attitude? What is the connotation of the underlined words?)

Some <u>well-intentioned</u> nations want to provide <u>assistance and aid</u> to <u>less fortunate</u> countries. (What is the writer's tone? What is the writer's attitude? What is the connotation of the underlined words?)

Points of View

When you consider the tone of a piece or the tone you wish to take in an assignment, also think about the point of view—from whose perspective the piece is written. If a writer uses the first person, singular point of view ("I"), then he or she is talking from a personal perspective.

Example:

I remember my prairie childhood with affection.

If, instead, the writer chooses a first person, plural point of view, then he or she wants to include you, the reader, in the discussion. Of course, such a point of view is more intimate and makes the assumption that you are really part of the discussion.

Example:

We all want to try our best to raise money for the Society of Wayward Poodles. Sometimes "we" as a point of view can be condescending as in, "We all want to take our medicine, don't we?" The first person, plural can be patronizing as in, "We all want to own the best car on the road."

A third person, plural point of view is often the one recommended for writers. By choosing third person, plural ("they," "people," "students," and so on) rather than third person, singular ("each student should bring his lunch"), you will avoid sexism in your language. Sexism uses a particular point of view, usually male (as in "his lunch"), as if both genders share that point of view.

Examples:

All people have the right to personal privacy.

All students should bring their lunch to school.

Passive voice is a construction often used to report an event or occurrence. This point of view is selected if the person doing the action (the subject or agent) is not important, or if the writer wants to blur responsibility for action.

Example:

> The children were moved into another classroom in the school.

In the example sentence, the reader does not know who did the action. The important fact is that the schoolchildren were moved.

Sometimes authorities will use a passive construction to convey a "blameless" point of view.

Example:

> Gas prices were increased again today.

In this example, the reader cannot locate responsibility. Those answerable for raising and controlling gas prices are missing from the sentence.

Points of View

first person, singular	I
first person, plural	we
second person, plural or singular	you
third person, singular	he, she, it
third person, plural	they
point of view indistinct	often found in passive voice constructions

Example: The criminal was stopped at the border. (Who stopped the criminal?)

Exercise 4:   *Recognizing Point of View*

Work in pairs. Read each of the following examples. Tell what point of view you recognize in each. Explain how the point of view works in the example. Be prepared to share your answers.

1. I love the way summer brings out casual clothing, relaxed meals, and a sense of fun.

2. Economic indicators are pointing to a drop in prices in the housing market.

3. "The Prime Minister, a specialist in calling in the locksmith after the horses had fled—the whole herd in fact—and the barn in ruins, ended the week with a great raft of ethics proposals for cabinet, leadership candidates, backbenchers and lobbyists. I think it is more than fair to ask: Why wait for the middle of his third term to institute what the public would have welcomed at the beginning of his first?" (Rex Murphy, Canadian Broadcaster)

4. Marshall McLuhan said, "Canadians are the people who learned to live without the bold accents of the natural ego-trippers of other lands."

5. "I read and learned and fretted more about Canada after I left than I ever did while I was home. I absorbed anything I could on topics that ranged from Folklore to history to political manifestos . . . I ranted and raved and seethed about things beyond my control. In short I acted like a Canadian." (Will Ferguson, *How to Be a Canadian*)

6. Three people were arrested on Thursday at the main gates of the Montreal airport's main loading dock.

7. The Canadian beef industry estimates it has lost $7 billion since the Canadian–U.S. border was closed due to mad cow disease.

8. It is time for all of us to roll up our sleeves and get our annual flu shots.

9. A person needs to decide whom he should elect for the position of president of student council.

10. You must understand our return policy does not permit us to accept an item after 14 days of purchase.

Exercise 5:   Identifying Tone

In each of the following passages, identify the writer's tone.

1. Use these two general categories: formal and informal.

2. Then try to be more precise by adding another descriptor like "angry," "upset," "playful," "hopeful," and so on.

3. Underline words that helped you to recognize the author's tone.

4. What is the predominant point of view in each passage?

5. Be prepared to explain your answers.

6. Check with the Answer Key.

Passage 1:

Each Saturday morning at this time of year, my neighbourhood observes the ritual known as Getting Rid of Stuff. Front lawns teem with relics from attics and basements: orphaned plates, dented toys, jackets with killer shoulder pads, and a turntable with the hopeful sign "Still works!"

Strolling past with my grocery bags, I marvel at the useless junk some pack rats have hoarded for years. Then I remember my own hoard: the mouldy vaporizer, the half-dozen maps of San Francisco (one per trip because we never arrive prepared) and a cocktail dress in a screaming shade of fuchsia, last worn when Madonna and Sean Penn were still an item.

There's more, but you get the idea. While my neighbours purge their flotsam and jetsam, mine explodes from every drawer, which means I'm hopelessly behind the times. This is, after all, the golden age of organizing, when the ultimate status symbol is a pristine closet full of storage bins in fashion colours, and the virtues of "conquering clutter" fill websites, magazine layouts and entire TV shows.

Source: Rona Maynard, "My Cluttered Life," Chatelaine *Jul. 2005: 40.*

Passage 2:

Architecture is a knowledge-intensive business. When clients retain the services of an architect, they seek knowledge ranging from aesthetics to technical know-how to effective relationship-building skills. Firms compete on the basis of how clearly they understand stakeholder priorities as well as their insight in ways that far exceed standard "we listen to you" marketing promises.

Source: Sharon VanderKaay, "The Business of Selling Knowledge, Part 1," The Canadian Architect *Feb. 2005: 27.*

Passage 3:

Robert Louis Stevenson said: "Life is not a matter of having good cards, but of playing a poor hand well." To stress proof our children, we need to teach them how to play poor hands well. One of the best ways is to show them how to take something stressful or negative and look at it in terms of advantages and opportunities, or in some way to see it in more positive or very neutral terms. This is called "reframing."

The person who learns how to quickly reframe stress will feel more empowered, regardless what obstacles life places before them [sic]. Even the most severe stress, perhaps caused by an accumulation of losses, can be the source of incredible personal and spiritual growth for them. They will feel those losses, and will certainly grieve them. More importantly, eventually they will find a way to use those experiences to enhance and enrich their lives.

Here's an example of reframing I found a few years ago (source unknown): A man and his two young children were riding a city bus late in the afternoon. The children were constantly running up and down the aisle, yelling at each other. The man seemed oblivious to their activity. One woman was bothered by their behavior, and tapped the man on the shoulder. She said, "Don't you see that your children are bothering the other passengers?" He replied, "Oh, yes, I guess they are." He paused, and with tears in his eyes said: "We just came from the hospital. Their mother died an hour ago, and I don't know how to comfort them." The woman instantly perceived the situation much differently, and was no longer bothered by the children's behavior.

Source: Judy Neal, "Making Diamonds: Helping Children Benefit from Stress," Natural Life *Mar.–Apr. 2002: 21. Reprinted by permission of Judith M. Neal, M.A.*

Exercise 6: *Tone*

Using each of the following topics, write a sentence or two, expressing the tone shown in parentheses after each topic. Bring your answers to class and be prepared to share them with others.

Example:

shift work (informal, negative):

Working the late shift at the hospital creates constant disruption in my home life and keeps me "out of synch" with the rest of the world.

1. your wages (informal, positive)

   _____

   _____

2. your wages (formal, negative)

   _____

   _____

3. health (informal, ironic)

   _____

   _____

4. city government (informal, satiric)

   _____

   _____

5. home entertainment systems (formal, angry)

   _____

   _____

6. choosing a career (formal, hopeful)

   _____

   _____

7. fashion (informal, playful)

   _____

   _____

8. cooking (formal, authoritative)

   _____

   _____

9. parents (informal, respectful)

_____

_____

10. skiing (informal, ironic)

_____

_____

Where Do I Find Ideas?

How do writers get ideas? Once you have selected something of interest that will please both you and, with any luck, your audience, you must create some ideas. Prewriting involves preparing to write. Usually, writers start by thinking about what they have to say, but they find it is not always easy to come up with ideas. Writers use strategies; some they have learned along the way, but many they have borrowed from other writers.

Generating ideas means using techniques and tricks to find or invent ideas so that you have some raw material to work with. Use a variety of methods to assist you in creating thoughts for your writing since the same strategy does not necessarily work in all situations.

How to Generate Ideas

Writers will tell student writers to develop some techniques and personal habits. Writers use a variety of techniques. Some fiction writers keep notebooks for ideas. Barnaby Conrad, author of over 24 books, says, "If you, as an embryonic writer, are not keeping notes regularly, you deserve the guilty feeling that is oozing into your body right now" (_Writer_, June 1992, 9). Other writers like to haunt bookshops and hang out near magazine stands. They claim that looking over the pages and spending time browsing reading materials gives them lots of ideas.

Writers who like to work with the Internet can also peruse a wide range of websites, searching for items of interest. You might be one of these writers. However, you must use caution not to borrow too freely from pages on the Internet. All writers must respect copyright: They must not plagiarize others' written materials. However, all writers can certainly learn by reading other writers' works.

Tips for Generating Ideas

As in other situations in life, good tools are important. However, you can have excellent tools but not know how to use them. It is the techniques and applications that make you better at using tools. When you write, the better tools you have to get the job done and the more techniques you have to use them, the easier the writing job becomes. It is critical that you do not "get stuck" in writing assignments because you do not have the right tools at hand. Tools for writing are really strategies to use when you realize you are not moving forward with the job.

BECOME A READER AND LEARN TO RESEARCH   Writers gets lots and lots of ideas from reading. Writers learn about writing by reading other people's work; they also gain ideas from reading widely.

In " How I write," Anne Rice says this about where she finds ideas: "The best come from my research. I read nonfiction, history, archeology, and some New Age material about people who claim to see ghosts or have had near-death experiences" (*Writer*, Feb. 2001).

Canadian film-maker Atom Egoyan, director of such award-winning films as *The Sweet Hereafter*, attributes his career start to some early reading and research he did when he was a high school student. He claims his first film instruction book came from his high school library in Victoria, British Columbia.

FREE-WRITING   Free-writing is a term used to describe a technique for creating ideas. To free-write means to allow yourself to write freely, without constraints of any sort, on a topic of interest to you. As you free-write, you begin to understand what you know about something. You start to recognize if you do have something to say. To free-write, try using the following steps:

Steps to Free-Writing

- Choose a topic of interest amongst those assigned.
- Choose a place to free-write where you will not be interrupted.
- Choose five or six fresh sheets of paper or open a new computer file.
- Have a watch or clock available to view as you write.
- Look at the time and write it down on a piece of paper beside you.
- Since you will write for 20 uninterrupted minutes, add 20 minutes to the start time, and write the stop time in large numbers underneath your starting time. Write "STOP" beside the second number.
- Write in a continuous fashion for 20 minutes. Do not stop keyboarding or writing.
- Write anything that comes into your mind on the topic—anything at all. Do not censor yourself. Do not stop to think about your writing. Do not correct anything. Keep writing for 20 continuous minutes.
- When you reach the "STOP" time, cease writing.
- Rest for a few minutes.
- Reread what you wrote.
- Select ideas of interest by underlining the words, using a brightly coloured highlighter pen. Put the ideas that seem to go together into a group; this is called clustering and is a useful method to help you see how ideas may connect.
- On a fresh sheet of paper or in a new computer file, write down the ideas you have highlighted.
- Look over your new list.
- Save the list as an ideas file. Give the computer file a distinct and easily recognizable name.

Example:

Imagine someone wants to write about buying a computer. The writer has chosen to free-write for about 15 minutes. Below are the notes from the imaginary writer's free-writing session.

Topic: Tips for Buying a Computer

I've got a fixed budget of $2000. What about the power of the processor? What brand name? Should I worry about the brand or not? I should think about the size of the RAM and the system speed, especially if I'm going to run games—a huge memory-eater! Speaking of a graphics card...Maybe I should use my own experience. I can talk to others; Blake is my favourite techno-geek; he has tons of information. I can read what's on the Internet and pay attention to some blogs. Sometimes there are pretty good reviews, too. I can check the flyers and talk to salespeople, maybe even do some tryouts in the store. I guess I should figure out my main purpose for computer use and users—they always ask you that in the store—who's going to use it? I should take my time and not make a rush purchase. I know good bargains come up in back-to-school September sales and Christmas sales.

Notice the writer does not use complete sentences and does not pay much attention to grammar and punctuation. Free-writing is not an assignment you will be marked on—it's for your own personal use to help you with your writing ideas. If you do decide to share it with another person, he or she should understand these are "thinking notes"; they are not your best academic prose!

DRAWING Many writers find that drawing helps them to develop ideas. You need not worry about your beliefs about your artistic talents. Remember, you are not trying to develop drawing skills: you are attempting to develop thinking skills. You are drawing in order to help you think.

You can use diagrams, geometric figures, lines, squiggles, boxes, faces, or whatever else seems interesting to use. For example, think of a map. Isn't a map really a way of thinking about a concept? After all, the world does not really look the way a map does, but its hills, distances, terrain, sub-structures, and so forth may be represented by a map. As you know, there are many kinds of maps that are designed for different purposes. A navigational "map" is not the same as a road map. A treasure map is not the same as the "map" of the shopping mall.

The map or drawing you make may also serve different purposes. You may draw one map to help you "see" the overview of something, like the plot of a story, for instance.

Another map may help you understand the relationship between characters. For instance, a novel may have a complex set of characters who develop a variety of ways of relating to one another. Planning a piece of writing by drawing out the relational lines and then examining those lines in detail may help you to visualize your project in a new way. Some people have used a tree drawing with the trunk as the main idea or thesis, larger branches as main points, and smaller branches as examples, proof, evidence, or other support. One writing student drew a geometric figure: The base was a flat plane, representing the central idea; a number of equilateral triangles represented each paragraph, with the base of each triangle as the topic sentence, and the corners of the triangle as the "structure" of each paragraph: the major points. If you like to draw, try using your skill to draw your plan, rather than using words. You might be very satisfied with the results.

Exercice 7: Drawing Ideas

Take each of the following topics or assignments and "draw your way through" to some ideas. Be prepared to show your "drawings" to others, to talk about the drawing, and to explain how the drawing helped you.

1. You have been assigned this topic: Men and Women in Professional Sports.

2. You have been assigned this topic: Pluralism in Canadian Society.

3. You have been assigned this topic: Canadian Television.

KEEPING A RESPONSE OR DOUBLE-ENTRY JOURNAL   A response journal is somewhat different from an ideas book. A response journal is a means of keeping notes as you read. Sometimes these journals are called "double-entry" journals because you divide the page in half: One side of the page is a place for you to record your ideas, thoughts, feelings, drawings, diagrams and incidental notes as you read. The other half of the page is for you to record what the writer says. Here is where you would record direct quotations, paraphrases, and short summaries, with appropriate page numbers. The response journal is useful in three ways:

1. It gives you a place to jot down responses to an idea or author's words.
2. It gives you a place to collect an author's words, thoughts, and ideas.
3. It provides you with a permanent set of notes which will become more and more valuable to you over time. You can keep all of the response journals you make and file them away by date. Having an archive of your own response journals will be valuable to you in a number of courses.

You needn't spend a lot of time and money on response journals. Buy a packet of the cheapest notebooks you can find. Always have one on hand as you read. Date each entry and take the two types of notes as you read. What a worthwhile source these journals will become!

Example of a Response Journal
Response Journal: Entry: May 12, 2005
The Life of Pi by Yann Martel, Vintage Canada, 2002.

My Responses and Ideas	*Writer's Words*
• I like how the writer starts his story about how difficult writing is and how he had to struggle to get over the fact that his novel wasn't selling. It must be hard to face that fact. Maybe he thinks, "My writing isn't very good—nobody likes it!" Maybe he is experiencing a "crisis of confidence"; I think all writers must go through that, me included!	• He says "readers ignored it" (v).
• He also talks about how that lack of confidence spills into his next writing project.	
• Well, he may have lost confidence, but at least he keeps his sense of humour!	• Martel says, "I mailed the notes of my failed novel, I mailed them to a fictitious address in Siberia, with a return address, equally fictitious, in Bolivia" (vii).
• I am starting to really like the humour in the book. I'll have to pay attention to how Martel uses it. What role will humour play?	

USING DISCUSSION   An excellent way of checking your understanding and perspective on an issue is to debate it with a friend or a group of friends. Many people feel very comfortable if they can verbally express their ideas. In fact, you may be the sort of person who likes to "talk out" ideas with someone else.

Discussion can be a great way to help express and clarify underdeveloped notions. Engaging in a lively verbal exchange with someone else, particularly someone who is interested in the topic, can be really stimulating and motivating. A good example of discussion groups at work today is book clubs. Today thousands of book clubs meet every week online and in person across Canada and the United States.

Healthy and respectful debate should also be part of your life as a student and as a citizen. Suppose, for instance, you have a strong interest in public housing and are planning on becoming an urban geographer, a city planner, an architect, a social worker, or a civil engineer. Perhaps you choose this topic as a research project. You might find other students with similar interests who might want to meet and discuss issues relating to public housing. Interested individuals usually speak passionately about their topics, and often, along with information, are good sources of inspiration.

You might even decide to form a discussion group, particularly if you are working collaboratively on a group project for a course. Small group projects can be very rewarding, or they can be a disaster. Frequently, having some ground rules to foster discussion can be helpful. When everyone agrees to follow the "rules," then discussion can flow in a civil manner without egos getting in the way.

GROUND RULES FOR DISCUSSION   Ground rules are guidelines that everyone agrees to follow in a discussion. Your group may decide to add others to the list below:

- Do not interrupt someone when he or she is speaking.
- Do not insult the speaker because you do not agree with the speaker's point of view.
- Be sure you understand the speaker's points. Ask for clarification of a point if you do not understand it.
- Be respectful to speakers in the group.
- Stick to the topic.
- Ask questions to help clarify understanding.

When your group first meets, the members may decide to appoint one member as the "watchdog," the individual who calls someone when he or she is breaking one of the agreed-to rules. As members of the group become more familiar with one another, the watchdog will no longer be a necessary role.

Exercise 8:   Discussion as a Tool

Follow these directions for a small group discussion. Your instructor will assign five or six topics.

1. Select one of the topics.

2. Gather together with others who have also chosen the same topic. Remember, you should have three to five members in your group. If there are not enough members, choose another discussion group.

3. Use the ground rules for discussion.

4. Go to another part of the campus for your discussion. The classroom gets very noisy when too many people are talking at the same time. Your instructor will tell you how much time you have for your discussion.

5. When your discussion is ending, talk with others in the group about the discussion itself. Was it worthwhile? Did you follow the ground rules? Did the discussion help you gain ideas?

6. When you return and the class reconvenes, be prepared to share your reactions to the discussion with the whole class.

Review Test

Try the following review test. It will help you assess what you have learned from the chapter. Be prepared to share your responses with others in the class.

Part 1: Without looking back in the text, write definitions for each of the following terms.

1. prewriting _____

2. procrastination _____

3. tone _____

4. point of view _____

5. free-writing _____

6. ideas book _____

7. response journal _____

8. audience _____

9. passive construction _____

10. connotation _____

11. satire _____

12. irony _____

Part 2: Name three points of view.

1. _____

2. _____

3. _____

Part 3: Give three tips for generating ideas.

1. _____

2. _____

3. _____

Part 4: Writing sentences with different tones and points of view.

Write a sentence for each tone and point of view asked for in the following.

1. You are a new student at the University of Bravo. You write a letter to the Dean of Student Affairs because you want to volunteer for her new committee: Making Campus Life Better. Write a sentence that expresses your reasons for wanting to join the committee. Write from a first person perspective.

   _____

   _____

   _____

2. You want to write for the student newspaper called Campus Spoof. You are asked to write a satirical article about the food in the cafeteria. Write a sentence from your article. Write from a third person point of view.

   _____

   _____

   _____

3. You are writing a paper for your English class. Your paper is about the high cost of getting a university or college education. In one of the paragraphs, you want to have an ironical point of view. Write from a third person, plural point of view.

   _____

   _____

   _____

Assignment

Do an Internet search on how writers write. Choose one writer who interests you. Read online what the writer says he or she does to prepare to write. Answer the following questions and bring your answers to class:

1. How does the writer select a topic or theme?

2. How does the writer generate ideas?

3. What does the writer say about preparing to write?

4. Are there special circumstances the writer needs to have in order to write?

5. What likes and dislikes does the writer mention about his or her writing preparation?

6. What does the writer say about writer's block?

7. What tips or techniques did you pick up from the writer?

Bonus Exercise: Tone

Find a short article of interest about fashion using the Internet or a current magazine. Read the article. Underline words that convey the author's tone. Consider the point of view. Then write a paragraph of 150–200 words on how the tone works in the article. Bring the article and your work to class. The instructor will ask you to post your article and writing in the classroom. You and the rest of the class will circulate to read the articles and student writing. The class will then discuss what students learned about writing from the assignment.

CHECKOUT

Here are some of the ideas you will take away with you after you have completed the chapter:

1. Complex writing tasks, like research papers, will require more preparation while simpler or shorter tasks will require less.

2. Free-writing is meant to help you generate new ideas.

3. Prewriting is a stage wherein you think and prepare to write.

4. Interest is a motivator; as you write, visualize your reader, imagined or otherwise.

5. Discuss your writing ideas with friends.

6. Be on the lookout for writing ideas; try using a pocket notebook.

7. Journal writing can be extremely beneficial.

8. Break free of procrastination by taking control of your learning.

chapter 2

Writing Phases: Planning to Presentation

Chapter Objectives

What will you have learned when you have completed this chapter?

You will be able to

1. put together a plan for your next writing project.
2. decide which organizing tools are best for your writing tasks.
3. work with drafting to develop your ideas into a written, organized form.
4. recognize that revision is necessary in your writing.
5. consider editing and proofreading skills as part of the writing process.
6. benefit by presenting your writing assignments correctly.

Introduction

Despite the fact that some writers make writing sound and look "easy," writing takes a lot of planning if you want your writing to be good. Good writers plan what they are going to say. Their writing may seem flawless to you—it flows, is well organized, captures your interest, and has many exciting ideas. You can only see what the writers have produced; you cannot see what the writers have gone through to get there.

Planning can take many different forms and is connected to purpose. If you want to build a house, you will need blueprints to express your plans. If you are presenting ideas to your colleagues at work, you will need to condense your points and highlight the important ones. You might choose Microsoft PowerPoint or another software program like it as the means to put your presentation together, but you will have to plan each slide carefully, using point form. Whatever your project may be, the planning you choose should suit the project.

As a writer, you also have choices of planning tools, depending on your project. A major term paper requires a much more extensive planning tool than a short-answer writing assignment does. Of course, to start planning, you will need to gather some ideas through prewriting as you learned in Chapter 1. Once you get some ideas, what do you do with them?

Self-Test

Read each of the following statements. Decide if each statement is true or false. Write T or F in the spaces provided. Check your answers with the Answer Key.

1. A formal outline is only used for formal pieces of writing. _____

2. A formal outline contains main ideas only. _____

3. An informal outline sketches out your ideas. _____

4. An outline is an organizing tool. _____

5. A draft means a version of a paper. _____

6. Revision means I only have to make small changes in the writing. _____

7. The first draft should include editing. _____

8. Macro-level revision means I revise larger features of the paper. _____

9. Micro-level revision means I revise at a sentence level. _____

10. I should start with micro-level revisions. _____

11. Peer editing includes evaluation of another student's draft. _____

12. MLA style refers to guidelines to documentation—how to show sources. _____

13. All instructors require a title page with your paper. _____

14. Proofreading includes work on changing the organization of a draft. _____

15. The final presentation must include an outline. _____

Phase 2: Planning

Academic writing requires organization. When you are assigned a project or paper, you will notice it usually includes using a variety of elements. These components might be your ideas, your research notes, and a particular format. You must combine these elements effectively, and that requires planning.

Some Organizing Tools

Writers have preferences about which organizing tools they like to use. Some writers say they do not like formal outlines but prefer less formal or sketch outlines to help guide their writing. Other writers suggest that formal outlines are the best organizers for them because ideas are clearly mapped out in detail. Although writers differ on their choice of organizing tools, they all agree: Ideas must be organized well in advance of the actual writing. Organizing tools are essential to writers.

Writers also recognize that outlines can be changed because writing is a recursive activity, not a linear one. Recursive means repeating the process as needed in order to achieve a satisfactory outcome. Outlines provide structure to the organization of a piece of writing, but they should never be rigid or inflexible. As you work through your research and your writing, you may find new exciting ideas cropping up. You should feel comfortable adding these new ideas to your outline and, perhaps, even deleting others.

As an organizing tool, outlines are somewhat plastic: They can be shaped and moulded, depending on your purpose.

The Formal Outline

A formal outline is a popular, traditional tool. It uses a series of numbers and letters to indicate the level of ideas. Roman numerals I, II, III, IV, V, and so forth stand for major ideas. Capital letters A, B, C, D, and so forth represent main points. Numbers 1, 2, 3 appear as minor points under the main points. If you want a very finely detailed formal outline, you may use small letters, a, b, c, d, and so on to represent subpoints under the numbers. Underneath the subpoints (a, b, c, d), use small Roman numerals i, ii, iii, iv, v to represent the smallest details of all. When you construct a formal outline, write a single statement at the top of the page to indicate what the paper will be about. This statement is called the thesis statement. This sentence is the most important one because it frames your discussion—what will be included in the frame and what will be left out. In the essay chapters of this book (Chapters 4 and 5), you will learn more about thesis statements and how to frame them. For the purposes of outlining, however, your thesis statement can be quite fluid because you are just in the planning phase of your paper. You may find as you gather ideas and make an outline that you want to adjust or rewrite your thesis according to what changes emerge.

Review the formal outline below. Then answer the questions that follow it.

Thesis: The Harry Potter series by J. K. Rowling has been the biggest publishing success of the last 100 years.

I. Astonishing sales (MAJOR IDEA)
   A. Global (MAIN POINT)
      1. over 250 million copies sold (MINOR POINT)
      2. translated into 47 different languages
   B. U.S. market
      1. 102 million copies sold
      2. thousands of Harry Potter groups and websites
   C. Canada and the U.K.
      1. Bloomsbury, British publisher of the Harry Potter series, says 750 000 copies of *Harry Potter and The Half-Blood Prince* were pre-ordered before the release date.
      2. Raincoast Books has the exclusive publishing rights in Canada and has sold more Harry Potter books than any of the other bestsellers in Canada combined.

II. Success of the author, J. K. Rowling
   A. Financial
      1. received $105 000 for first in the series, *Harry Potter and the Philosopher's Stone*
      2. told not to expect too much more
      3. now on Forbe's list of the world's richest people
   B. Personal
      1. came from being a poor, single mother
      2. manages her personal fame well
      3. believes that reading enriches children's lives

III. Creation of new marketing strategies
   A. Use of the Internet to sell books online
      1. millions of copies sold through Amazon
      2. cross-referenced on hundreds of thousands of websites
   B. Fan pages on the Internet
      1. thousands of fan clubs
      2. "fanzines"
      3. wizard clubs online
   C. J. K. Rowling's strategy of dealing with the press
      1. no personal promotions necessary
      2. has meetings with fans, and media are invited
      3. includes children in all promotional materials

Exercise 1: Questions on the Formal Outline

Answer each of the following questions. Be prepared to share your answers.

1. How many paragraphs do you expect the writer to write using this formal outline?

   _____

2. How many main points are there in the first paragraph?

   _____

3. What are the minor points of the first paragraph?

   _____

4. How many major ideas are there in the second paragraph?

   _____

5. What are the main points of the second paragraph?

   _____

6. How many major ideas are there in the third paragraph?

   _____

7. What are the minor points of the third paragraph?

_____

8. What tone do you think the writer has chosen?

_____

9. What do you think of the writer's plan?

_____

10. Do you think the formal outline will produce a good piece of writing?

_____

Exercise 2:   Making a Formal Outline

Imagine you are writing an article on party planning. Construct a formal outline to show your overall content and organization. Your instructor may ask you to hand in your outline.

The Informal Outline

An informal outline is much more sketchy than a formal outline. It may just be a list of broad headings like this:

- Harry Potter series
- sales success
- success of the writer J. K. Rowling
- new marketing strategies introduced

You may also use boxes, circles, or other geometric figures of different sizes. Large boxes could represent the major points; smaller boxes the minor ones. You can arrange an informal outline so that only a few items show, perhaps just the major ideas.

THE SKETCH A sketch outline is a type of informal outline. A sketch outline is only seen as a starting point for writing, unlike the formal outline which has already been well planned out. A sketch outline might look something like this:

- what about the Harry Potter series?
- how many copies in the series have sold?
- why?
- what about the writer, J. K. Rowling?

The sketch outline above gives you something to use as a starting point. As you research and write, you may find your ideas take shape and become slightly different than you originally anticipated. As you work, your sketch outline fills out. After working with it for a short time, you might decide to construct a more fully developed, formal outline.

Other Planning Tools: Checklists, Questions, Notes

Some writers like to work with even less formal tools. Checklists are simple but can be quite effective, too. Checklists can be a series in a form like this:

Harry Potter Series

British origin
the author
the sales
marketing strategies
the reason for popularity
the reader

You might start with a list of ideas you have researched on a topic of interest. You can then check the ones you want to use in your writing and start from there.

Other writers recommend using a set of questions. The questions can also be used to guide your research. You may then select the ones with the richest information and ideas and use them to write from. Your set of questions may look something like this:

- Who is J. K. Rowling?
- Why are her books so popular?
- Who reads them?
- How many books have sold?
- Who markets them?
- How are the books marketed?
- Who owns the publishing rights in Canada?
- What about the movies based on the books?

These organizing tools, formal and informal, are not demanding to use. The informal ones are wonderful for you to use after you have done some thinking, prewriting, and research. Very quickly they will help you get started writing. You can construct more formal outlines after the prewriting phase, as long as you feel you are ready to do that. Instead, you might use a sketch, checklist, or set of questions as your first organizer, and a formal outline after you've had a chance to see how the "flesh" of the ideas fits on the "bones." After you've done some preparation work with prewriting strategies and you've used some organizing tools, you are ready to write your first draft.

Outlining as a Study Tool

Organizing tools like outlines are indeed useful for your writing, but did you know they can help your studying? You can use formal outlines and even informal ones to chart how written material has been organized. Understanding the organization of something develops your comprehension of the material. The speed and depth of your reading comprehension will depend on how familiar you are with the texts of a community. Since you have so much material densely packed with information to read for your courses, you will benefit from being able to use learning and thinking tools in a variety of ways. Outlines can really help your study reading.

Example

Read the following text:

> Life stages affect how individuals and their families cope with illnesses and injuries. Lifespan development theory states that each individual will go through a sequence of orderly, distinct stages in life. At each stage, a person has to master some developmental task. Each task is a growth responsibility that appears at a certain stage of an individual or family's life, and has emerged from biological needs, cultural imperatives, and family goals. These tasks must be successfully completed in order to secure present satisfaction, social approval, and future success. Failure to do so will result in dissatisfaction, social disapproval and difficulties with later tasks and life. Because individuals and families interact, individual and family life cycles often juxtapose and intertwine with each other. Understanding life-cycle theory can help the physician to assess and intervene appropriately.

> *Source: Vincent Poon and Ed Badner, "Life-Cycle Theory: Make Use of It in Your Practice,"* Patient Care *Mar. 2005: 62.*

Formal Outline for Use as a Study Guide

The following example shows one way study notes, using an outline and the paragraph from *Patient Care* could be organized. This outline is not the only way the ideas from the passage could be organized. However, the outline helps the reader to know if he or she has understood the passage. Besides, the clear set of outlined notes will make an excellent study aid.

Notice that the writer has included a list of unfamiliar terms used in the passage. When it comes time to study, the student can glance over the list of terms to check understanding of them. Also notice that there is only one major idea (I. Lifespan development theory), with three main points (A, B, C) and several minor points (1, 2, 3, or 4) beneath each main point. Because this passage has only one paragraph, it will not have a thesis statement, but it will have an overarching major idea.

I. Lifespan development theory
    A. Everyone goes through a sequence of separate life stages
        1. these stages affect how we cope with crises
    B. What is involved in the stages?
        1. each stage includes a "developmental task" of some sort
        2. each task furthers growth
        3. each task comes from biological, cultural, or family needs
    C. What results?
        1. successful task completion ensures satisfaction
        2. non-completion of developmental tasks leads to social difficulties and later life problems
        3. contrasting life cycles in individuals can complicate family life
        4. physicians who understand lifespan development theory and the cycles can assist individuals and families

Key Terms: lifespan development theory, cultural imperatives, juxtapose, intervene

Exercise 3: *Making an Outline from a Reading*

Use the above example as a model. Construct a formal outline, based on the passage provided below. Also include a list of unfamiliar terms at the end of your outline. Your instructor may ask you to hand in your outline or may have you share it with others.

First Nations are the largest of the three constitutionally recognized Aboriginal peoples in Canada. Within Manitoba, the Cree (mid north and north), Dakota and Assiniboine (southwest), Dene (far northwest), Ojibway (south) and Oji-Cree (mid northeast) are the indigenous peoples of Manitoba who have contributed greatly to the economy and vitality of Manitoba and Canada through community and individual achievements, traditional and westernized knowledge, philosophy, arts, science, and culture. First Nations do share a belief in a holistic balanced approach to life as necessary to maintain good health. Yet the diversity of language, culture, geography and history of the 63 First Nations communities necessitates their full involvement in changing policies and approaches in health.

According to the Statistics Canada Aboriginal Peoples Survey 2001, the Manitoba First Nations population is 107,146, which is approximately 10% of Manitoba's total population with 47% of First Nations people living on reserves. The remaining 53% live in rural communities, often close to their reserve communities, or in urban centres. The median age of Manitoba First Nations people is 22.8 years, while that of the non-Aboriginal population is 38.5 years. Thus, First Nations planning for future employment and services must consider that this youthful population "bulge" is a decade behind the mainstream population. While mainstream society is concerned with preparing for the retiring baby boomers' needs, including housing for "empty nesters" and senior homes, First Nations are planning for more schools and family housing.

Source: M. MacKinnon, RN, Grand Rapids Cree Nation, "A First Nations Voice in the Present Creates Healing in the Future," Canadian Journal of Public Health *Jan.–Feb. 2005: 513–514. Reprinted by permission of the Canadian Public Health Association.*

Phase 3: Drafting

You will often hear the term "drafts" associated with phases of writing. *Drafting* is the development of ideas into a written, organized form: It entails writing several versions, called *drafts*. You will work through the process from draft 1, the initial draft, to the final draft. Different assignments may require a different number of drafts, depending on how complex the assignment is and how familiar you are with the texts and resource materials relating to the discipline. If, for example, you have never written a literature paper before, you can expect to write more drafts than usual. Even if you have written a literature paper but have not completed one on poetry, you will be learning as you go. Anticipate doing extra drafts.

All writers use drafts when they write. Some writers work with fairly detailed out-lines, even at the first draft phase. Others like to move freely with their ideas through the first draft in order to see where the writing ends up. If you are a person who is comfort-able with a more freewheeling style, then you may get your best results from a kind of free-writing approach to the first draft. However, if this idea makes you tense or fearful, use a sketch outline to write your first draft.

Bear in mind that drafting means a series of attempts. Your first draft will not be your final because ideas need to be developed over time and through effort. You might see drafting in writing like this: Ideas follow an arc—you start with ideas, and then you move forward with them, writing as you go along until you reach a peak in the process where-by thoughts and ideas begin to slow down; at this point you stop. Then you begin to review your first completed draft. You cannot actually predict how long or wide the writ-ing arc will be, but sometimes you can make a good guess based on how difficult the assignment is and how at ease you are with the material.

When you are drafting, you are composing or getting ideas down on paper. You are not editing or revising. Composing means you should feel relaxed and allow the ideas to spill out onto the page.

Writing the First Draft

Writing your first draft should be a fairly enjoyable experience, if you have planned for it. After you've done some prewriting work, chosen an organizing tool, and have a plan for writing, you can begin with some confidence. Remember, your first draft is your first attempt, not your last.

Begin writing the first draft as soon as you can. Having ideas down on paper in a developmental form is important. Following are some tips for writing your first draft:

1. Gather all the materials you will need: your notes, your plan for writing, notepaper, pens, and so forth.
2. Try to set aside one uninterrupted hour to start.
3. Find a quiet and relatively private space. If your home is a busy, noisy place, stay on campus for an extra hour and work in the library or learning centre. Some writers can work in a noisy, busy place, but most people find a library, a private study space, or a quiet room at home works best to enhance, not distract, concentration.
4. Work either on computer or on paper, whichever is more convenient and comfort-able. Double space your work, so you can add ideas.
5. Begin to write, according to your plan. Keep writing. Don't stop until your hour is up.
6. As you write, do not concern yourself with errors. Don't stop to correct spelling, grammar, or punctuation. Don't worry a sentence to death. If you stop often, you will interrupt the "flow," and flow is what composing is all about!
7. After the hour is over, stop for a break.
8. When you return to your draft, you may want to keep writing.
9. When you feel that you have finished the entire first draft, stop.
10. Save the file and then print a copy of what you have written, if you have worked on a computer.

11. Review what you have written. Use a pen or pencil in a bright colour and add notes here and there in the draft as you read. The notation may be as simple as an asterisk (*) to indicate a section needs revision. It may be an underlining that shows a sentence needs work. It may be a comment in the margin. Use the first draft checklist that follows to help guide your review.

12. Pack up all your notes, the printed draft, and your other materials, and leave the task overnight or for a few hours. It is important to begin the second draft with fresh eyes.

Other Drafting Tools

Having a variety of tools is most beneficial. A checklist is a marvellous device because it is so flexible and simple, yet so effective. You can have lots of different checklists for lots of different purposes. The checklist below is for you to use as you are reviewing the first draft of an assignment. You can develop your own checklists that you custom fit to your own needs. If you like to compose on the computer, then the second tool may be a useful drafting tool for you.

First Draft Checklist

I have met the assignment objectives.
I have a clear beginning.
I have provided clear points.
I have included some convincing examples.
I have good variety in my sentence structure.

Using Computers and Multiple Drafts

If you prefer to write, i.e., compose and edit, using a computer, then you probably have already learned a number of writing strategies. However, some of the following tips may be new to you and may prove to be useful.

1. Each time you write a draft, open a new file. This practice will prevent you from overwriting. Open a file and call it, "Draft 1, an abbreviated title, and the date." Save it the same way, but make sure your title is not too long. The next time you return to the computer to write, open Draft 1, copy it, and then paste it to a new file. Save the file as "Draft 2, same abbreviated title, and the date." You will have a number of drafts in various files at the end of your writing, but, in this way, you will never lose any of your work.

2. Make a backup of your work. Use a flash device or some other portable means for the backup. If your hard drive dies unexpectedly or if your computer becomes infected, you have backed up your work and can use another computer to continue with your projects. Often students save only to the hard drive. Usually they have no technical problem with this situation, but some do. It is completely heartbreaking, frustrating, and angering to lose all your work, so take a little time and back up your projects!

3. Always keep a hard copy of every assignment you turn in. Hand one in to your professor or instructor, and keep the other one on file. Sometimes, papers are mislaid. If you have a hard copy at the ready, you will be able to turn in a misplaced assignment. Of course, if your assignment has been backed up in your computer files, you can always print another hard copy as needed.

4. Open another file for notes. Save the file as "Notes for _____ (abbreviated title of your paper.)" As you read, research, and take notes, you can place any useful idea in this file. It is doubtful you will use all of the notes and ideas, but, should you decide to use one, you will know where to look for it. You can continue to add comments as you work through your assignment. Do not delete these files because some of them may be useful for more than one course.

5. Keep files up to date. Manage your files well, and the work will seem easier. Keep your files focussed: Don't try to do too many things with one file. Instead, create a folder for each assignment. In the folder, put all of your draft files and your note files, along with anything else relating to the assignment.

Phase 4: Revising

Samuel Johnson said, "What is written without effort is in general read without pleasure." His comments capture why writers revise, but sometimes student writers have a mistaken impression of what revising a written composition means.

Some students think revising equals repairing a few sentences, running their work through a spell checker, and adding fancy title pages with catchy titles in appealing fonts. Nothing can be further from the truth. Surprising as it may seem, revising is one of the most important phases of writing, yet many students resist the need to revise.

Perhaps they have run out of time—the deadline peeks just around the corner. Perhaps they are so tired of the paper, they cannot bring themselves to rethink it and make any major changes to it at all. Perhaps they cannot evaluate their own work very efficiently. Students can change all of these circumstances by better planning and by opening their hearts and minds to other ways of doing things.

Revising is the critical process of evaluating your work in order to improve it.

The process looks something like this:

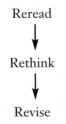

Reread

Rethink

Revise

Why Revise?

The prefix "re" looms large in these words: It means "again"—read again, think again, and work again. Revising is so important that if you do a good job of it, your assignments will likely receive good grades; if you do a poor job or make no effort at all, your mark will reflect your lack of effort. Moreover, learning to revise will help you become a better writer.

It is at the revising phase that writers can go "back" over their work to read it as a whole, judging how a piece "sounds." They mark parts that sound unconvincing, are badly worded, seem illogical, look out of place, appear unsupported, or lack effectiveness. They rework these parts and then, if needed, adjust the whole.

They also consider if the piece matches their initial purpose and intended audience. Does the work answer the assignment? Does it have the tone, structure, argument, evidence, and overall organization that will make it effective and convincing?

Finally, be sure to allow time in your schedule for the revision of papers. Plan to revise. Even if you have only a few hours to spend revising, you will be grateful that you did: You will catch errors, rework parts of your paper that might have proved embarrassing, and generally, pull the piece together for a better presentation and mark!

Levels of Revision

Although experts may not agree exactly how many levels of revision are possible, they will agree on three types. In *Spotlight on Critical Skills in Essay Writing*, these levels are called macro-level (large-scale), micro-level (smaller-scale), and editing. You will read more about editing in the next section. For the time being, consider what comprises macro-level and micro-level revisions.

MACRO-LEVEL REVISING　This revision includes the whole paper. You reread the paper to discover its overall strengths and weaknesses. You note areas where more evidence is required, where an additional step must be added, where a conclusion does not follow, where an idea needs clarification, and so forth. Then you rewrite sections, tailoring them to the rest of the paper. Finally, you reread the paper again to see if the improvements you've made are satisfactory.

MICRO-LEVEL REVISING　This type of revising has to do with a particular section of your paper. Perhaps you notice that the body of your paper is strong, but your conclusion is weak. You reread the paper, paying particular attention to the conclusion. Then you spend extra time reworking the conclusion to give it what you want: a sense of summary and a sense of closure with some punch. You then reread the paper, seeing what the new conclusion "sounds like."

Checklists for Revising

Macro-level:
My paper answers the assignment.
My paper has a consistent tone that I like.
My paper addresses a certain audience.
My paper has an effective overall arrangement.
My paper is well-developed with good support overall.
My paper is convincing.

Micro-level

My paper has an effective and interesting introduction.

My paper has a clear thesis or organizing statement in the introduction.

My paper has clearly developed and well-supported body paragraphs.

My paper has few faults in logical thinking.

My paper presents lots of good evidence: examples, explanations, statistics, or reasons.

My paper has an effective and forceful conclusion.

Getting Feedback

Feedback means having others read your work and gathering their comments and suggestions in order to improve the piece of writing. At the same time, you will also be improving your general skills as a reader. You may see two types of feedback used in courses: peer reviews or peer editing, and self-assessment.

PEER REVIEWS   Peer reviews or peer feedback means having other members of the class read your work and comment on it. You, in turn, will do the same. Most of the time, instructors provide criteria for peer reviews to give focus to the reviewers' comments and to make them as constructive as possible to the writer receiving the review. Often peer reviews include written comments on a peer review form. After the peer review, you will be able to discuss the written comments with the reviewer. You can find many examples of peer review sheets on the Internet. Try downloading one and using it for one of your own papers.

Examples Taken from Various Peer Review Sheets

Is the writer's purpose clear?	yes	no
Does the writer have a clear thesis statement?	yes	no
Is the writer's tone appropriate?	yes	no
Has the writer provided sufficient support?	yes	no
Are points well developed?	yes	no
Do conclusions follow from the arguments presented?	yes	no

Sometimes you may ask a friend or relative to read your paper. Some outside reviewers can do a good job, providing you give them a list of criteria for the review. However, not all feedback is going to be useful. Value-laden criteria (the "goodness" or "badness" of something) does not offer you much help, unless the person using this type of criteria can provide you with clear reasons for his or her likes and dislikes.

In most cases, getting an outside reviewer is a good idea. The reaction to your paper is beneficial, in general. Common instances of useful feedback may include helping you to pinpoint confusing areas of your paper. For example, a reviewer may not understand what you are saying in a passage, although to you it may be perfectly clear. He or she may question you on the paper's organization, but you may have thought the paper was sensibly structured.

SELF-ASSESSMENT You can learn to be a good a good reviewer of your own work, but it takes some time, patience, and self-training to do so. You may find assessing your own written work is a bit more difficult than assessing someone else's. Why that is so may have to do with learning to be self-critical in a positive and constructive way.

Some Tips for Self-Assessment

- Keep track of your writing strengths and weaknesses. Most writers know what gives them trouble in the writing process. Each time you write a paper, try to recognize what is giving you trouble. Write it down in your ideas notebook. Work through the problem and write down the action you took.

- Keep track of the instructor's feedback. For example, if the instructor tells you to give more specific examples in a paper, make a note of that in your ideas book. Date the entry.

When you are revising, go back over the instructor feedback notes you have taken. Then check this feedback against your new work. For example, you might ask yourself, "Have I provided specific examples in this paper?"

- Develop your own checklist. For instance, if you know that you often forget to check your papers for effective conclusions, put "check conclusion" on your checklist.

- If you are serious about improving your writing, read what other writers have to say about what they did. Every year publishers produce collections of essays on writing by writers.

Exercise 4:   *Optional: Other Writers' Tips*

Try an Internet search for what other writers have to say about assessing their own writing. Can you find new words of wisdom to guide you in your reflections of your own work? If you find useful tips or strategies, bring them to class. Be prepared to share them with others.

Phase 5: Editing and Proofreading

After you have completed a number of drafts, done some macro- and micro-level revising, and satisfied your checklists about organization and content, you are ready to edit. Proofreading means looking for errors in the paper, usually at the sentence level. You can now consider the mistakes in sentences—grammar, usage, spelling, and punctuation.

Your instructors and professors will expect you to have proofread your papers well before handing in the final drafts. Without a doubt, you will lose marks if you have not proofread your work. More importantly, concise and clear written communication means a great deal in the professional world. Poor editing results in bad impressions.

Grammar and Usage Errors

Do you know which errors plague you? Do you have trouble with subject-verb agreement, parallelism, verb tenses, or pronoun references? Do you forget certain forms of verbs? Writers know what kinds of difficulties they have with grammar and usage. However, in order to improve, you have to do something about the errors—namely, eliminate them!

Keep track of which mistakes you tend to make in your papers. When you edit and proofread, print a hard copy of the paper. As you read, pay attention to the errors particular to your writing. Read each sentence out loud. Highlight any sentence with an error. Try to read for one type of error at a time. In other words, if you have some problems with subject-verb agreement, for example, then read through your paper, looking only for s-v agreement mistakes. What this tells you is that you will have to read your paper several times for editing and proofreading purposes. Chapter 14 in *Spotlight on Critical Skills in Essay Writing* offers a close look at some of the common sentence-level errors. Pay particular attention to this chapter as it can help you overcome some of your mistakes.

Spelling Errors

Some spelling errors can be repaired by running your paper through the spell checker in your word processing program, but this practice does not always guarantee all mistakes will have been removed. Although you should use the spell-check, do not rely on it completely. The spell-check program cannot read context. In other words, it cannot tell which spelling is appropriate because it does not comprehend subtle differences in the use of a word. If you have trouble with synonyms in spelling (words like "there," "their," and "they're"), then you cannot rely on spell-check to help you make corrections.

Remember that some instructors penalize heavily for spelling errors in papers. They believe students should know how to clean up spelling by using spell-check, a dictionary, or a proofreader.

Punctuation

All college and university writers need to learn how to use English punctuation correctly, particularly commas, semi-colons, apostrophes, and quotation marks. Read your paper line by line, looking for errors in punctuation. If you are not sure if there is an error in a sentence, ask someone. Look up punctuation usage on the Internet; there are thousands of sites, particularly those hosted by colleges and universities.

Invest in an excellent English handbook. Many new versions appear every publishing year. Get used to using the handbook. When you don't know how to use a mark in punctuation, look up its use in the handbook. The more often you look it up, the more likely you are to remember the correct usage.

Pay attention to the details of punctuation. Your message can be misleading or inaccurate if your punctuation is off. Instructors and professors will deduct marks for punctuation errors.

Chapter 14 contains some information on common punctuation errors.

Phase 6: Presentation

The last phase of the writing process is the presentation of your paper. Presentation means the font you should use, the format of the paper, the title page (if one is required), the line spacing, the pagination, and the overall appearance. You want to make a good impression, so be sure your presentation does that. The presentation also sets a tone: It shows your attitude to the assignment. If you have spent quite a bit of time and given lots of effort to the first five phases of writing, you will want to complete your project on a high note—a polished and pleasing presentation.

The Final Draft

The final draft means the version ready to be handed in for reading and evaluation. It is the culmination of all of the efforts of the previous drafts. Before you submit your paper, proofread one final time. Surprisingly, you will catch some errors you missed previously.

THE FIRST PAGE OF THE FINAL DRAFT　Some instructors or professors want to see a title page as the first page of your final draft. However, if you are preparing a paper according to MLA style (Modern Language Association), you will not produce a title page.

THE TITLE PAGE　Following is a sample title page. Your instructor may ask you to produce a title page slightly different from the sample. If your instructor has handed out special instructions regarding the title page, you should follow them to the exact detail. Most instructors are very particular about students' following correct format.

Use an 11- or 12-point clear font. Do not use any font larger than that, and do not use a script type of font. Most instructors do not want the assignment to be submitted in a presentation folder. Instead, staple the paper together in the upper left-hand corner.

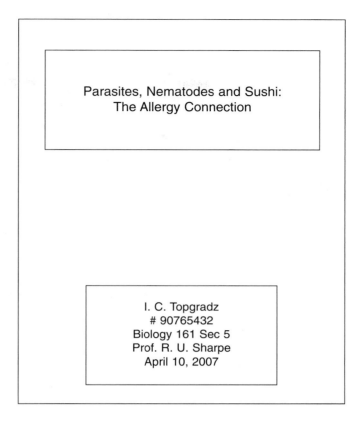

- About three inches from the top of the page, centre the title of your paper. Be sure the title shows the focus of the paper. If the title in the above example had been: "Parasites and Nemotodes," it would have been too broad. It would not reveal the specific focus of the paper. The title as given above shows the paper's clear direction. All words in the title must be spelled correctly.

- About one inch from the bottom of the page, type your name, your student number, the name of the course and your section number, the name of your professor or instructor, and the date the paper is due. (Do not date the paper the day you complete it; date it the day you hand it in.)

MLA-STYLE FORMAT   MLA-style format has specific requirements. English courses and most humanities courses use the MLA (Modern Language Association) style of formatting and presentation. You will read more about MLA-style papers in Chapters 11–13.

Below is a sample of the presentation format of an MLA-style paper. Generally speaking, MLA papers do not have title pages.

- The title should show the focus of the paper. If the title in the example below had been: "Characterization in W. O. Mitchell's *Who Has Seen the Wind?*" it would have been too broad. It does not reveal a specific focus. The title as given below shows the paper's clear direction by relating specific concepts.

Polly Pepperpot
ID 507999325
Prof. U. B. Tokswell
English 161 Sec 5
November 4, 2007

Pepperpot 1

Natural Optimism: Folk Wisdom and Characterization in W.O. Mitchell's
Who Has Seen the Wind?

- Use a running header on the upper right-hand side of the page, showing your last name and the page number.
- On the first page about one inch down in the upper left-hand side, key in your name, your student number, the instructor's or professor's name, the course and section number, and the date of submission.
- On the first page, centre your title about a half inch below the date of submission. Do not put the title on every page.
- Double space the paper.

Review Test

Define each of the following terms in one or two sentences. Use separate paper.

1. informal outline

_____

2. revision

_____

3. feedback

_____

4. title page

_____

5. micro-level revision

_____

6. draft

_____

7. peer editing

_____

8. formal outline

_____

9. final draft

_____

10. proofreading

_____

Assignment

Select one of the activities below for your assignment. Be prepared to hand in your work.

1. Choose either one of the readings listed below; find it in Chapter 16, "Readings"; and prepare a formal outline of its structure. Use the guidelines to formal outlines given in this chapter.

   Reading 18: "Four Hundred Years of Fantastic Literature in Canada," by John Colombo

   or

   Reading 11: "Sea Urchins and Sand Dollars—No Brains but Lots of Sense," by Julie Johnson, Pat Haugh, and Susan Taylor.

2. Prepare a formal outline for an essay on one of the following topics:

   - Hiking
   - Child Care
   - Smoking Salmon
   - Blogs
   - Kids and Being Street Smart

3. Develop an informal outline about a popular television series.

Bonus Exercise: *That or Which?*

Use "that" to introduce a restrictive clause—a clause necessary to a sentence because it helps to define the subject of the sentence. It clarifies which subject. Use "which" to introduce a non-restrictive clause—a clause not necessary to defining the subject. A "which" clause adds information not really needed in the sentence. It does not clarify the subject.

Use commas with non-restrictive clauses. Do not use commas with restrictive clauses.

The house that burned was built in 1912. (Restrictive: It defines which house specifically.)

My salmon sandwich, which was wrapped in plastic, tasted delicious. (Non-restrictive: The clause adds information but is not needed.)

Add "that" or "which" to each sentence below. Check your answers with the Answer Key.

1. The alarm _____ sounds like a whistle wakes the baby every night at eight.

2. *Oryx and Crake*, _____ is speculative fiction, is Margaret Atwood's eleventh novel.

3. Mimi prefers to eat low-fat snacks, _____ she prepares herself.

4. The steel table _____ has only two legs should be sent to the junk pile.

5. Mr. Taki bought blue and white wallpaper, _____ was on sale, to use in the small dining room.

6. The accident _____ claimed the victim's life occurred at this intersection last Thursday morning.

7. The conference on eco-globalism, _____ was held in Helsinki in 2006, had over 5500 delegates.

CHECKOUT

Here are some of the ideas you will take away with you after you have completed the chapter:

1. Organizing tools help you get started writing.

2. Writing is a recursive activity.

3. Feedback is useful for developing revision checklists.

4. An effective Internet search can display helpful writing tips.

5. MLA-style format has specific requirements.

6. Think of the writing process as having six phases in order to take a step-by-step approach.

chapter 3

The Paragraph

Chapter Objectives

What will you have learned when you have completed this chapter?

You will be able to

1. describe the important elements of an academic paragraph.
2. recognize the purpose of a topic sentence.
3. construct a clear topic sentence.
4. provide effective supporting ideas for your paragraph.
5. write an effective wrap-up sentence for your paragraph.
6. recognize the use of transitions.
7. use transitions in your paragraphs.

Introduction

A paragraph, the most important element in your academic writing, is a collection of sentences centring on one major idea. The paragraph is unified when every sentence in it develops the *topic sentence*—the sentence that contains the main idea of the paragraph. Usually the topic sentence is the first sentence in academic paragraphs because it lets the reader know immediately what the paragraph will be about.

Each paragraph contains *major points* that support the topic sentence. In every paragraph, you should provide three major points (occasionally two major points may be enough) that support the main idea in your topic sentence. You must fully explain and develop each of your major points with *supporting details*: examples, reasons, statistics, anecdotes, research, or experiences. Your purpose in academic writing is usually to explain, inform, or convince. The more well thought out each of your paragraphs is, the more likely you will achieve your purpose in writing. To add coherence to your paragraph, use transitions between major points. *Transitions* are words, phrases, or sentences that act as bridges between ideas. They make the writing style more fluid.

Each paragraph should end in a satisfactory manner: It wraps up the discussion in a sense, while, at the same time, it should lead to the next major idea in the discussion—the next paragraph of the essay or composition. The last sentence of a paragraph in an essay does a kind of transitional work and is called a *transitional sentence*. Transitional sentences help ideas flow nicely for the reader because the development of ideas is moved along logically and smoothly.

Self-Test

To check out your knowledge of paragraphs, answer the following questions. Check your answers with the Answer Key at the back of the book.

1. What is a paragraph? Give a definition in no more than two sentences. Write it here.

   _____

   _____

2. What is the main idea in a paragraph?

   _____

   _____

3. What is the topic sentence in a paragraph?

   _____

   _____

4. What is a supporting detail in a paragraph?

   _____

   _____

5. What could provide support for an idea?

   _____

   _____

6. What is a transition in a paragraph?

   _____

   _____

7. Writing topic sentences.

Write a topic sentence for each of the following topics. Discuss any aspect of the topic you wish. Since there will be many variations in the answers, the Answer Key will provide only a few samples. Your instructor may ask you to check these answers together.

a) television programming

   _____

   _____

b) modern farming

_____

_____

c) breaking a bad habit

_____

_____

d) preparing for an exam

_____

_____

e) choosing a daycare centre for your child

_____

_____

Outlines

An outline is a blueprint for your writing ideas and is one of the most useful writing tools you can find. Basically, you can use one of two types: the full sentence outline or the point form outline. Use full sentences for all of the points in your paragraph in the full sentence outline, while, in the second type, use short notes rather than full sentences. In either case, write out your topic sentence in full.

Example: Sentence Outline

Topic sentence:
Deadbolts are the most effective locks for home security.

Major point 1:
These locks have a square-faced bolt.

Support major point 1 (explanation and a statistic):
The shape of the bolt prohibits the forcing open of a door with a knife blade, screwdriver, or similar instrument. (explanation)
According to a June 2006 Canada Council for Safety report, deadbolts proved to be a deterrent in 95% of home entry attempts by thieves. (statistic)

Major point 2:
These locks have a longer bolt, usually one inch.

Support major point 2:
The longer bolts make the door virtually impossible to pry open because of the tight closure; there are no gaps between the door and the frame. (explanation)

Conventional night latch locks often leave a gap, allowing for "credit card" entry robberies. (example)

Major point 3:

Some deadbolts provide extra security for French doors by locking from the inside with a key.

Support major point 3:

The homeowner locks the deadbolt from the inside by the turn of a key. The homeowner can then remove the key, and even if the burglar breaks the glass, he or she cannot open the lock. (explanation)

Wrap-up and transitional sentence (if inside an essay):

The many advantages of a deadbolt make it a good investment for a homeowner; however, the type of door frame is another consideration in home security. (wraps up the ideas and leads to the next paragraph in the essay)

Example: Note-Form Outline

Topic sentence:

Deadbolts are the most effective locks for home security.

Major point 1:

- square-faced bolt.

Support major point 1 (explanation and a statistic):

- shape prohibits the forcing open of a door with a sharp instrument. (explanation)

- June 2006 Canada Council for Safety report deadbolts deterrent in 95% of burglary attempts. (statistic)

Major point 2:

- a longer bolt, usually one inch.

Support major point 2:

- door impossible to pry open because tight closure; no gaps between the door and frame. (explanation)

- night latch locks leave gap, allowing for "credit card" entry robberies. (example)

Major point 3:

- extra security by locking from inside with key.

Support major point 3:

- locks the deadbolt from the inside by a key, can then remove key, and burglar cannot open the lock. (explanation)

Wrap-up and transitional sentence (if inside an essay):

- advantages of a good investment; however, door frame is consideration in home security. (wraps up the ideas and leads to the next paragraph in the essay)

Example Completed Paragraph:

Here is the completed paragraph. Please note the writer has added transitions between the points to add emphasis, new ideas, and flow. The transitions are shown in italics.

Deadbolts are the most effective locks for home security. *To begin with*, these locks have a square-faced bolt. The shape of the bolt prohibits the forcing open of a door with a knife blade, screwdriver, or similar instrument, *for example*. According to a June 2006 Canada Council for Safety report, deadbolts proved to be a deterrent in 95% of home entry attempts by thieves. *Furthermore*, these locks have a longer bolt, usually one inch. The longer bolts make the door virtually impossible to pry open because of the tight closure; there are no gaps between the door and the frame. Conventional night latch locks often leave a gap, allowing for "credit card" entry robberies. *In addition*, some deadbolts provide extra security for French doors by locking from the inside with a key. The homeowner locks the deadbolt from the inside by the turn of a key. The homeowner can *then* remove the key, and even if the burglar breaks the glass, he or she cannot open the lock. The many advantages of a deadbolt make it a good investment for a homeowner; *however*, the type of door frame is also a consideration in home security.

Exercise 1:   *Developing an Outline*

Choose one of the following topics. Develop an outline—either in sentence form or note form—using the topic you have chosen. Write out your topic sentence in full. Be prepared to hand in this assignment or have a peer from class evaluate your work. Your outline should be easily transformed into a paragraph. Be sure to include three major points to support your topic sentence.

1. raising horses

2. employment programs for youth

3. building your own gazebo

4. problems with bills

5. easy credit

6. rock climbing

7. online magazines

8. recreational snorkelling

9. family vacations

10. extreme sports

11. urban camping

12. wine tasting

13. computer animation

14. herbal teas

15. financial investments

Structure of a Basic Academic Paragraph

Your academic paragraphs should look like this:

Topic sentence (contains the main idea of the paragraph)

↓

First major point (in a separate sentence)

↓

Support for first major point (proof or explanation in separate sentence or sentences: use examples, reasons, statistics, research, anecdotes, or facts)

↓

Second major point (in a separate sentence)

↓

Support for second major point (proof or explanation in separate sentence or sentences: use examples, reasons, statistics, research, anecdotes, or facts)

↓

Third major point (in a separate sentence)

↓

Support for third major point (proof or explanation in separate sentence or sentences: use examples, reasons, statistics, research, anecdotes, or facts)

↓

Wrap-up sentence (logical closing to the paragraph and leads to the next paragraph as a transitional sentence or device)

Developing Topic Sentences

The topic sentence expresses what the paragraph will be about—in other words, its main idea. Usually you find topic sentences placed at the beginning of paragraphs. It is most important to write clear topic sentences that direct both you and your reader through the writing. Topic sentences control the scope of a paragraph, so do not make them too broad or too general in nature. By the same token, do not make them so narrow that they are really a supporting detail rather than a major idea. If your topic sentence is too narrow, you will not have anything much to discuss in the paragraph.

Examples:

Topic sentence too broad: Government should be investing in alternative sources of energy.

Topic sentence too narrow: Switchgrass on the Canadian prairies is a useful source of ethanol.

Topic sentence is workable: The Canadian government should investigate the potential of using ethanol as a new energy source.

Exercise 2:   *Topic Sentence Development*

Work in pairs. Tell whether the topic sentence is workable, too narrow, or too broad. Be prepared to provide reasons for your answers.

1. Caribou have a terrible smell.

2. Most of the students at Rona College like to participate in rollerblading sports.

3. Although the SmartCar is proving to be popular, it does not provide an alternative for most consumers.

4. Baseball, unlike soccer, relies on the mental agility of its players.

5. Wayne Gretsky is a really important figure in hockey.

6. Nine out of ten participants chose Flako pastry made from no transfat margarine.

7. Cordless tools have their drawbacks.

8. Orange and pink are a horrible colour combination.

9. The police in Toronto have learned a good deal from the London police based on their experience of the terrorist attacks in London in 2005.

10. No child should have to go to bed hungry.

11. This sleeping bag uses the marvellous new material, microheat, as an insulator.

12. The children from the grade four class of Roseberry Elementary learned three important lessons about helping others.

13. Marijuana laws need to be updated.

14. Aboriginal leaders have four claims in the North Battleford, Saskatchewan, area.

15. Cruelty to animals is outrageous.

Exercise 3:   Developing Topic Sentences

Write a clear, effective topic sentence for each of the following. Your instructor may ask to see your work or may ask you to share your work with others.

1. making a difficult decision

_____

_____

2. studying sharks of the North Atlantic

_____

_____

3. escorting a friend to court

_____

_____

4. owning your own business

_____

_____

5. making perfect muffins

_____

_____

6. selecting a birthday gift for your partner

_____

_____

7. selling real estate

_____

_____

8. choosing a college or university

_____

_____

9. preparing an effective resumé

_____

_____

10. talking to your children about stealing

_____

_____

Exercise 4: *Peer Editing Topic Sentences*

Form a group of three to five people. Make three to five copies of the topic sentences you developed in the previous exercise. Exchange them with members of your new group. Edit these sentences together by examining each topic sentence according to the following ideas:

1. Is the topic sentence workable or is it too broad or too narrow? Why?

2. What ideas would you expect the writer to include in his or her paragraph?

3. What advice could you give to help the writer improve his or her topic sentence?

Developing Support

Support means providing evidence or proof for your major points. The more specific and convincing your evidence, the more likely it is you will persuade your reader in some sense. You can build support in a number of ways.

- Provide more explanation:

    State your point. Then in the sentences that follow, elaborate or explain the point.

    Example:
    Historically, pandemics begin in very isolated regions and take quite a number of years to spread. (major point) In other words, diseases that are communicated by human or animal contact do not infect huge areas or populations suddenly. (supporting explanation)

- Provide examples, statistics, or facts:

Example:

Historically, pandemics begin in very isolated regions and take quite a number of years to spread. (major point) In other words, diseases that are communicated by human or animal contact do not infect huge areas or populations suddenly. (supporting explanation) For example, the World Health Organization names six stages in the development of a pandemic, with each stage taking some time to progress.

- Provide a reason or a chain of reasoning:

Example:

Historically, pandemics begin in very isolated regions and take quite a number of years to spread. (major point) In other words, diseases that are communicated by human or animal contact do not infect huge areas or populations suddenly. (supporting explanation). Viruses are found in ducks, chickens, whales, seals, pigs, and horses, but according to the World Health Organization, only birds host all subtypes of influenza virus. The virus can be transmitted directly from the animal or the animal's environment to humans, but often, there is an intermediate animal host. Pigs, for instance, can act as the intermediate host, so the virus travels from the bird, to the pig, to humans. By this time, however, health protection intervention will have stopped the mass transmission among humans. (chain of reasoning)

Exercise 5:   *Providing Support*

Work in pairs or small groups. You will see major points given in the exercise below. Provide the type of support asked for in each item. Write down your answers, and be prepared to share them with others in the class.

1. Major point: Skateboards on city streets are annoying.

   Support: Provide a chain of reasoning. _____

   _____

   _____

   _____

   _____

   _____

2. Major point: Teen marriages are not generally sanctioned in the Western world.

   Support: Provide a fact or statistic. _____

   _____

   _____

_____

_____

_____

3. Major point: Positive body image is stronger among young males than females in North America.

   Support: Provide a fact or statistic. _____

   _____

   _____

   _____

   _____

   _____

4. Major point: Recreational activities bring families closer together.

   Support: Provide more explanation. _____

   _____

   _____

   _____

   _____

   _____

5. Major point: Mutual sympathy and open communication engenders community.

   Support: Provide a chain of reasoning. _____

   _____

   _____

   _____

   _____

   _____

Exercise 6:   *Providing Reasons*

Provide three reasons that support each of the following. Your instructor may ask to see your work. Be prepared to share your answers.

- Three reasons why procrastination can harm a student.

    1. _____

    2. _____

    3. _____

- Three reasons why having a brother (or sister) is important.

    1. _____

    2. _____

    3. _____

- Three reasons why video games are so popular.

    1. _____

    2. _____

    3. _____

- Three reasons why I love going to parties.

    1. _____

    2. _____

    3. _____

- Three reasons why I should get an A in my English course.

    1. _____

    2. _____

    3. _____

Unity

Unity in your paragraph means that every idea you provide in the paragraph relates to its central theme or main idea. All of the ideas in the paragraph contribute to the topic sentence (which states the central or main idea of your paragraph).

As you think of new points and support in your paragraphs, think of how they relate to the topic sentences. Do they relate? Are they on topic or not? If they are not, then your writing will be disjointed to the reader.

Coherence

Coherence in your paragraphs involves the linking of your ideas. Each part of the writing connects to the others, so the overall writing has a logical sense to it. Coherent writing has a flow of ideas and style. You may consider unity as part of coherence since unifying all ideas will make pieces of writing flow logically.

To add to the coherence in a paragraph, use transitions. Transitions like *furthermore, also, on the other hand, consequently,* and so forth provide direction to your idea flow. They tell the reader, "Now I want to add to that," or "Now I want to contrast that," or "Now I want to leave that point and start another." The next section discusses transitions and their uses.

Using Transitions

Transitions are words, phrases, or sentences used to express a change of ideas. One idea might be ending and another idea beginning. They can show relationships between ideas in terms of time, logic, or explanation. The next section reviews the kinds of transitions at your disposal as you write.

Transitions to Show Emphasis or Addition of Ideas:

1. and	6. in addition	11. again
2. also	7. moreover	12. further
3. finally	8. furthermore	13. to begin
4. as well as	9. in the same fashion	14. first, second, etc.
5. too	10. another	15. next

Example Paragraph 1:

My neighbours just purchased a really unusual new dog, a Hungarian Puli. Its appearance is a little startling at first. Poldi, the Puli, has an amazing coat, which seems to have the ability to form dreadlocks unless it is combed. Moreover, the dreadlocks hang in long rope-like strands, giving the dog a distinctive, almost Rasta look. In addition, the thick dread coat makes it difficult to tell which end of the dog is which. My neighbours' children love to walk Poldi so that they can trick passersby into patting the wrong end of the dog. Also, the Puli's floppy style of walking and running emphasizes its long corded coat.

Transitions to Show Time Order or Chronological Order:

1. first	11. now	21. third
2. in the first place	12. eventually	22. next
3. second	13. at last	23. during
4. later	14. after that	24. when
5. then	15. early	25. finally
6. last	16. whenever	26. after
7. until	17. in due time	27. prior to
8. as soon as	18. before	28. meanwhile
9. while	19. to begin with	
10. soon	20. afterwards	

Example Paragraph 2:

Making dill pickles is a relatively easy task. <u>First</u>, the cook should choose the freshest ingredients possible: pickling cucumbers about 3–4 inches long, pickling salt, spring water, fresh dill heads, and vinegar and pickling spices. <u>Next</u>, the cook should scrub each cucumber with a soft brush under cool, running water. It is important to keep the water flushing over the cucumbers to rinse away bits of dirt and debris. <u>After that</u>, the cook should select appropriate canning jars; one-half quart sized, wide-mouthed jars are most suitable. These jars are easy to pack with a single row of cucumbers. Of course, the cook must sterilize these jars in hot, boiling water. If the cook is using a fermentation method where the pickles cure by fermenting over a period of a few weeks, <u>then </u>he or she should put $\frac{1}{2}$–1 tablespoon of pickling salt and one dill head into each jar before packing in the cucumbers. The cook may add one clove of fresh garlic for flavour, too. <u>Next</u>, the cook pours spring water over the cucumbers, leaving about $\frac{3}{4}$ inch headspace at the top to allow for the slight bubbling occurring over the fermentation process. If the cook is going to water bath the pickles, he or she should prepare a pickling liquid of 5% vinegar, water, salt, a bit of sugar, and pickling spices. <u>As soon as</u> the liquid has come to the boil, the cook can pour it over the packed pickles in each jar, and <u>then</u> seal the jars and water process them for 10 minutes. The cook may wish to add another dill head to the top of the jar <u>before</u> sealing each. <u>After</u> the pickles have been processed for 10 minutes, the cook can remove the jars and cool them on a rack. <u>Finally</u>, the cook can label the jars and place them on a shelf in a cool, dark place. <u>Afterwards</u>, the cook feels a sense of satisfaction in looking over the jars of delicious homemade pickles that were so easy to make.

Transitions to Show Contrast or Difference:

1. but	7. opposite	13. even though
2. in contrast	8. on the contrary	14. different
3. however	9. on the other hand	15. than
4. yet	10. nevertheless	16. whereas
5. despite the fact	11. otherwise	17. conversely
6. although	12. still	

Example Paragraph 3:

Unlike the honeybee, a beneficial insect, the yellow jacket is considered a pest by most people. It is considerably more aggressive than the honeybee and can sting repeatedly. The yellow jacket is interested in garbage and protein materials early in the season and fresh fruit in the fall. In contrast, the honeybee is only interested in flowers. It will not pester people for their food at picnics, opposite to the yellow jacket. Even though both the honeybee and the yellow jacket belong to the same genus of insects, their food, social habits, and nest building activities are widely different.

Transitions to Show Similarity or Comparison:

1. both	5. respectively	9. in the same fashion
2. each	6. similarly	10. just as
3. like	7. also	11. compared to
4. likewise	8. and	

Example Paragraph 4:

Both porcelain and bone china are desirable types of pottery throughout the world. Known in various forms by most cultures of the world, each type is highly prized. Collectors comb the globe looking for rare and important pieces. Some are so valuable that only world-class museums or billionaires can afford them. For example, at Sotheby's Imperial Sale, held in October 2000, a fine Ming porcelain jar from the 16th century sold for $5,567,640. Likewise, both porcelain and bone china are held in high esteem because they are considered works of art. Artisans from different continents were employed specifically to hand paint elegant designs on vases, plates, and bowls. Even Picasso tried his hand at plate paintings. In the same fashion, china and porcelain are collected by millions as a hobby. Some of the most sought-after pieces depict famous historical scenes or moments. Great Britain, for example, commemorates its royal and historical figures of importance in china specially manufactured for a notable occasion. Prince Charles' two weddings, for instance, to Diana and then to Camilla, have been celebrated <u>respectively</u> in commemorative plates, dinner sets, mugs, teacups and saucers. After centuries, these two types of ceramics continue to be popular for their elegance, historic importance, and desirability to collectors.

Transitions to Show Cause and Effect:

1. as a result	5. accordingly	9. hence
2. consequently	6. so	10. if
3. therefore	7. to conclude	11. for this reason
4. thus	8. then	

Example Paragraph 5:

Watching the news before going to sleep can cause sleep disturbance or insomnia. The late-night news is often filled with depressing events. <u>As a result</u>, an individual is put into a kind of stage of alert. Images, sounds, or phrases may remain in a person's immediate consciousness, and <u>therefore</u> may plague the person as he or she tries to settle down and relax for sleep. <u>Consequently</u>, overstimulation and restlessness follow. <u>Thus</u>, a person becomes centred on worry and stress. <u>Accordingly</u>, the person becomes aroused rather than calmed into a state of sleep, <u>so</u> late-night news watching is not recommended.

Spotlight on Critical Skills in Essay Writing provides more information about transitions and transitional phrases and sentences. You can find additional sections by looking in the index at the back of the book.

Exercise 7:   *Using Transitions*

Work in pairs. In the following sentences, add a transition that would make sense for each sentence relationship. Pay attention to how the ideas in each sentence relate to one another. Be prepared to share your answers. Note that you may require a semi-colon in front of some transitions.

1. Dentists advise patients to floss their teeth; _____, they might suffer from periodontal disease.

2. Anwar enjoyed the tour of the museum, _____ he did not care for the meal in the cafeteria.

3. My sister claims that farmed salmon and wild ocean salmon taste the same, _____ I maintain the texture and flavour are different.

4. The force of the tsunami of December 26, 2004 was formidable; _____, it killed more than 150 000 people, which is _____ the entire population of cities like Barrie, Ontario, or Kelowna, British Columbia, in Canada.

5. Mieux-mieux, the long-haired cat, has a velvet cushion for her bed, _____, Boozer, the family dog, has to sleep in an old basket under the kitchen stairs.

6. Stilton Chesterson is the world's highest paid security chief, _____ he will not allow himself to be photographed due to the nature of his job.

7. _____ there is a heavy rain, we can hear foghorns as ships pass through the narrow passage between the islands.

8. _____, to start the engine, turn the key to the left; _____ hold down the green button for five seconds.

9. The muffins from that take-out restaurant are really high in calories; _____, they contain about five tablespoons of sugar each.

10. _____ Freemont had inherited a great fortune from his parents, he squandered his money on gambling and expensive cars, _____ within five years, he was destitute.

Exercise 8:   *Unity and Coherence*

Below is a paragraph that lacks both unity and coherence. Read the paragraph and answer the questions that follow.

Paragraph: Poor Unity and Coherence

Sports and fitness trends are related to what John Kelly, a University of Illinois sociologist, calls "the Olympic effect." Since the Olympic Games get such an abundance of media coverage and promotion, adult viewers tend to participate more just before, during, and immediately after the Olympics. The Olympics occur every four years. I do not tend to watch the Olympic Games coverage too much, although many of my friends do. After the Olympic flurry is over, participation in sports and fitness activities tends to spiral downward again, according to Dr. Kelly. However, casino gambling and poker have increased interest and participation since 2004. I do not gamble either.

1. Why does the paragraph lack unity?

Give some examples.

_____

_____

2. Why does the paragraph lack coherence?

Give some examples.

_____

_____

3. Does the writer use transitions or transitional phrases? Which transitions might the writer have chosen? Why? Give examples.

_____

_____

Point of View

Point of view means from which perspective a piece of writing is told. If you wanted to write about a childhood experience, for example, you would write using a *personal* point of view or using the first-person pronoun *I*. Most of your assignments at college or university will not ask for this point of view, but some instructors may encourage you to use it. Psychology essays, for instance, may ask you to talk about yourself in a particular situation as might cultural studies courses. Some instructors, however, ask you to avoid the personal or *I* point of view.

Keep in mind that different points of view serve different purposes. On occasion, you might find it is appropriate to use the first person, yet at others, first person is unacceptable. Your journal, for example, is written from a personal point of view, but your physics lab report is not.

What points of view are recommended in academic writing? Most of the time, you will write using a *third person point of view*, either *he*, *she*, or *they*. Use a third person, plural point of view if you want a non-sexist position. Since *they* does not name a gender, it tends to remove sexism from discussion. Also, *you* as a point of view is often discouraged. Some instructors regard *you* as presenting problems in writing because the writing style may seem sermonizing in tone. However, some instructors will allow the second person point of view, particularly if the writer must give instructions.

POINTS OF VIEW AND PURPOSES

- I (first person, singular) → the writer is involved in the events; the point of view is more subjective (personal involvement)

- we (first person, plural) → the writer and the reader are together involved in the events; the point of view is more subjective

- you (second person, singular or plural) → the reader is the focus

- he or she (third person, singular) → the point of view is more objective (at a distance) but a gender is named

- they (third person, plural) → the point of view is more objective (at a distance) but no gender is named

- one (third person) → the point of view is neutral. However, some instructors do not accept *one* as a point of view because it can make the writing style sound strained.

Check with your instructor about which points of view are acceptable in your assignments and which are not. Often your instructor will mention this information in your course outline.

Wrap-up and Transitional Sentences

You should end each paragraph in order to satisfy one of two purposes. First, if your paragraph is actually a composition or unit of writing that will stand by itself, use your wrap-up or last sentence to draw discussion to a close. You may summarize the main points of your paragraph, or you may simply restate your topic sentence. On the other hand, if your paragraph is part of the body of an essay, you will want to link this paragraph to the next one. Make the last sentence of your paragraph tie off discussion and lead your reader logically to the next main idea. In other words, last sentences of body paragraphs should be transitional, bridging between the paragraphs. Reread the five example paragraphs in the section titled Using Transitions, paying attention to the last sentence in each.

Review Test

Try this review test to see what you recall from the chapter.

1. Define a paragraph.

_____

_____

_____

2. What is the topic sentence of a paragraph?

_____

_____

_____

3. What is a main point in a paragraph?

_____

_____

_____

4. How can you provide support for your ideas in a paragraph?

_____

_____

_____

5. What is point of view in writing?

_____

_____

_____

6. Name the third person, plural point of view.

_____

_____

_____

7. Name the personal point of view.

_____

_____

_____

8. What is the purpose of a second person, plural point of view?

_____

_____

_____

9. What is unity in a paragraph?

_____

_____

_____

10. What is coherence in a paragraph?

_____

_____

_____

11. What are transitional words or phrases (transitions)?

_____

_____

_____

12. Name five transitions.

_____

_____

_____

Assignment

Write a paragraph of 150–175 words about one of the following topics. Start with a clear topic sentence. Use transitions in your paragraph.

1. babysitting

2. exercise classes

3. surfing

4. reading to young children

5. bingo

6. sewing your own clothes

7. getting tickets for a game

8. worrying too much

9. making a container garden

10. raising fish

11. going to the movies

12. working in a restaurant

13. saving money

14. keeping up with trends

15. grooming your dog

Bonus Exercise: *A Case of Who or Whom*

"Who" and "whom" are pronouns. As you may recall, pronouns are words that function as nouns and stand in for nouns. Pronouns can have three functions: They can be the subjects of sentences or clauses. They can be objects of verbs or prepositions. They can also show possession.

Examples:
Who knocked at the window?
The subject of the sentence is "who."
He gave whom some money?
The object of the verb is "whom."
Whose wallet is this?
The possessive case of "who" is "whose."

Hint:
Who is the subject case.
Whom is the object case.

Use the subject case after a linking verb.

Use the correct form of the pronoun to match its function in the sentence.

1. To _____ was he speaking at the dinner table?

2. We have decided _____ we will invite to the conference.

3. Ally and Samantha wish to know _____ you are.

4. The tourist sights are plentiful in Halifax and _____ knows best where to find them but my friend, Bert, _____ lives there.

5. It was Rico, I think, _____ was the best dancer in the competition held last weekend in Hamilton.

6. Mr. Daliwal consulted a lawyer _____ he met in Winnipeg during a business meeting.

7. Buster Keaton was the man _____ everyone loved in the silent movies.

8. The women, two of _____ are Finnish, told stories of their grandmothers.

9. To _____ do you turn in times of trouble?

10. Martial law was applied to those _____ were considered terrorists.

CHECKOUT

Here are some of the ideas you will take away with you after you have completed the chapter:

1. Full-sentence and point-form outlines are planning tools useful to writers.

2. Between supporting points, transitions promote emphasis and flow.

3. Transitions may be words, phrases, or sentences.

4. Last sentences of body paragraphs should be transitional.

5. The topic sentence of a paragraph shapes its main idea.

6. Major points provide arguments and evidence to support the topic sentence.

7. Most of the time, you will use a third person point of view in academic writing.

chapter 4

The Essay

Chapter Objectives

What will you have learned when you have completed this chapter?

You will be able to

1. write better essays by adopting a conventional academic essay form.

2. organize, clarify, and enhance your writing ideas by using rhetorical modes.

3. recognize that academic essays should be clearly, though not rigidly, organized.

4. adopt a thoughtful approach to the organization and presentation of all your writing.

5. write successful essays that attract and inform interested readers.

Introduction

Everyone agrees: Writing takes work. Stephen Leacock, a famous Canadian humorist, once said, "Writing is no trouble: you jot down ideas as they occur to you. The jotting is simplicity itself—it is the occurring which is difficult." The essay is the conventional form of expression in academic writing. Most of the courses in the humanities, social sciences, nursing, and business require essay answers. Although essays are commonly assigned to be written outside of class, in-class essay writing has become more popular during the semester and in examinations.

The following chapter introduces you to the basic form of the essay. You will learn throughout the course of this book to write more extended essays, too, in order to prepare you for the demands of your academic course work.

Self-Test

1. What is an essay?

   _____

   _____

2. What are the parts of an essay?

   _____

   _____

3. What is the purpose of the introduction?

   _____

   _____

4. What is a thesis statement?

   _____

   _____

5. What are transitions?

   _____

   _____

6. What is the purpose of the concluding paragraph of an essay?

   _____

   _____

What Is an Essay?

Definitions of an essay vary. One common definition for an essay is "a written composition on a specific subject." Another conventional definition adds another dimension: "an essay is a short, controlled composition giving the writer's views on a specific subject or expressing his or her opinions on a specific subject." Finally, you find another element in this definition: "an essay is a short composition that attempts to persuade the reader."

By amalgamating the definitions, you will have captured an essay's key components: "an essay is a short, controlled piece of writing expressing an author's views or opinions on a specific subject in an attempt to persuade the reader."

- short and controlled
- expressing views or opinions
- on one specific subject
- attempts to persuade

On first reading this, you might think that an essay is just a fancy name for a written argument, and in a sense, you are right. The term *argument* suggests controversial issues and clear reasoning. Although essays can deal with controversial issues in a reasoned way, they can also discuss a wide range of topics—from light and amusing to heavy and sombre—meant to convince readers. In other words, "Why cousins should not be invited to weddings" is just as much an essay topic as "Capital punishment should be reinstated in Canada." The first essay topic is not as serious in tone as the second, but it, too, is controversial. Both topics will try to convince readers of each writer's position or views.

Now you might ask: "What good will essay writing do me in my future career or studies?" Many courses in English, the social sciences, nursing, business and commerce, biology, engineering, history, philosophy, and so forth require students to explain and convince. Today companies are hiring new people based on their "soft skills," as well as their academic or technical training. Communication is a major component of a soft skills set.

Even in your daily life, you will do some writing that involves trying to convince somebody of something. If you write a letter of application, you are attempting to convince a prospective employer to hire you. If you write a letter to Bell Canada, complaining about a billing for unauthorized phone calls, then you are attempting to convince or persuade. If you have a dispute with your landlord or a car salesperson and you find yourself in court, the organization of your argument, written or spoken, will assist your attempt to convince.

Essay writing can become a useful learning tool to you in a number of ways. It can become a tool:

- to sort out what you think about some issue or topic.
- to convince others your points are valid.
- to organize written ideas.
- to coordinate and complete a thinking/writing project.
- to revise ideas.
- to incorporate others' advice about revision and improvement.
- to present a well-edited, thoughtful written piece.
- to gain the satisfaction that you are capable of all these things.

The Organization of Essays

Essays can have patterns of development called rhetorical modes or ways in which the information can be organized. *Spotlight on Critical Skills in Essay Writing* suggests five basic modes: process analysis, comparison and contrast, classification and division, cause and effect, and definition, all of which are discussed in more detail in Chapter 6. These modes are essentially the same as those you might use for writing paragraphs.

Of course, few people write essays by deciding first on the rhetorical mode and then on the topic. The rhetorical modes are simply tools. You can choose to use one or not. You will find that most writers use a blended approach: They may choose to compare and contrast two ideas, but they may also include the history of the ideas (process analysis or time order) and their impact (cause and effect).

Essays are a lot like people; each one you write will have its own *personality*. Some of your essays will fall into place easily, while others are stubborn and won't want to work for you. But our flexibility as learners allows us to accept the fact that things are not always the same. It is better to survey the tools in front of you, the essay designs, and choose one that seems to fit your taste and your purpose. You will write essays on various topics of interest to you, but your instructor will not ask you to write *pure design* types of essays. Some essays you write may contain a mixed pattern—a little cause and effect with a little contrast because this is what seems to work best for a particular essay. This makes sense, so don't panic: Mixing essay designs, unlike mixing drinks, has no ill effects.

You will see, though, that a clear directing sentence which contains the main idea of the essay is essential to you in the writing task. This sentence is called the thesis statement, and it controls the ideas and the organization of the essay.

Basic Structure of an Essay
Introductory paragraph with a thesis statement

↓

Body paragraphs with topic sentences, main points, and supporting evidence
(minimum of three)

↓

Concluding paragraph

You will write essays that have these same components. Academic essays have an introductory paragraph with a thesis statement—a main idea sentence controlling the whole essay. The body of your academic essay should have a minimum of three separate paragraphs, but more often than not, the body of an essay at the university level has more than three. Every body paragraph discusses a major idea of the thesis and develops points and evidence to support claims made by the thesis. The conclusion sums up the major ideas in the essay and leaves the reader with a general thought on the topic. Check with your instructor or professor about his or her preferences in essay writing. Some do not want a summary statement in the conclusion of a short essay.

An academic essay must have the following:

- introductory paragraph containing a thesis statement (controlling idea)
- body paragraphs (at least three that support the claims of the thesis)
- conclusion (summing up and providing a general thought)
- strong evidence
- good editing
- clear presentation (word-processed with title page, 11- or 12-point font, good spacing)

Purposes of Writing an Essay

1. To meet the requirements of a course or exam.
2. To provide a challenge in thinking an issue or topic through in an organized way.
3. To develop a sense of language.
4. To clarify thinking.
5. To develop intellectual powers using language.
6. To communicate an opinion or idea on a theme, special topic, or issue.
7. To provide a point of view on a theme, special topic, or issue.
8. To persuade readers to consider your point of view.

An essay can test and develop your skills in a variety of ways. Good written expression is one of the most important capabilities you can have today. Employers are looking for good communicators, not just those who are articulate and convincing in their speech, but those who are equally adept in their writing. As well, specialized writing like technical writing and persuasion have become fundamental to many colleges and universities.

As you write, you will make discoveries of different sorts. You will find out what you think about an issue. You will read what others have to say on the same topic. As a peer editor, you will read other students' work, and they may read yours. You will discover how you react to doing revisions and how you will incorporate suggestions and corrections into your writing routine. You will discuss ideas, and possibly debate them with a good deal of passion. You will find your own writing voice. You will surprise yourself at times, but in the final analysis, you will develop and improve as a writer.

An Overview of the Parts of an Essay

Academic essays are part of your writing life as a college or university student. You will need to know how to construct essays that are clear and convincing. The following section will provide you with important information about writing short prose compositions called "essays."

The Introduction

Your essay begins in a paragraph called the introduction. Your introduction should start in an interesting way. It should provide some background on your topic. You may choose to give your reader some general information on the topic in order to build a bridge of common understanding between you and your reader. Finally, end the introductory paragraph with a thesis statement. It expresses the main idea of the essay. It focusses on a topic and then angles it to show the author's point of view and usually the rhetorical mode of development—how you will develop and organize your ideas.

The Body

The body of an essay extends over several paragraphs. Each paragraph contains a major idea of the thesis and supporting points. It provides specific and convincing evidence for the major ideas. Sometimes you might have to do some research in order to provide convincing proof for the points in your paragraphs. The body should contain a minimum of three paragraphs, but, usually, it contains more. Each paragraph begins with a topic sentence, which controls the ideas in each paragraph.

Develop your discussion in each paragraph in a thorough way. Set out a point in a separate sentence; then provide proof, explanation, or other support for each point. The proof can consist of examples, quotations, facts, statistics, illustrations, or specific reasons. Balance each paragraph so that you discuss each point equally well. The body of the essay should show balanced discussion throughout the paragraphs. At the ends of body paragraphs, except the last, use transitional sentences—sentences that close one discussion and lead to another. These transitional sentences bridge ideas between the paragraphs.

The Conclusion

The conclusion wraps up the ideas of your whole essay. You may summarize the points to refresh them for the reader. End the essay by leaving the reader with a general thought on the topic. Try to have a forceful ending to ease the reader out of the topic. Remember that flat endings leave flat impressions. Do not introduce new ideas in the conclusion; instead, use the conclusion to tie off the ideas in the essay and to leave an impression on the reader.

Key Terms Connected to Essays

introduction	body paragraph	supporting evidence
conclusion	topic sentence	thesis statement
coherence	unity	narrative
expository writing	persuasive	rhetorical mode
editing	revisions	draft
outline	brainstorm	transitions
peer editing	documentation	

Starting the Introductory Paragraph: Brainstorm

One of the most difficult activities for all writers is getting started. Even the most experienced writers can have trouble putting the first words down on the page. You, too, may find this happening when you write. Try free-writing for a few minutes. Try drawing. Try opening a new file on your computer and writing without stopping for five minutes. Use a first sentence that begins like this: I'm having trouble getting started today. . . .

Consider the topic you have chosen. Usually you will be assigned a selection of topics to choose from. Select the one that interests you the most. Spend a few minutes thinking about the topic. Ask these questions:

1. What do I think I know about the topic?
2. What interests me about the topic?
3. What opinions do I have on the topic?
4. What experience have I had with the topic?
5. What do I need to know about the topic?
6. Should I do some research on the topic?

Exercise 1:   *Free-Writing to Generate Ideas*

Free-write for a few minutes on the topic of your choice. Use the above questions to guide you. Spend time thinking about your answers to these questions. Use brief notes. Work quickly so that you are moving along. Flow is important to the writing process. After you have spent some time making notes, try to write out a rough thesis statement. Be prepared to share your answers.

The Thesis Statement

The thesis statement is important—it is the engine in the machine, so to speak. Expository writing—writing that explains or informs—will comprise most of your writing assignments, but there will be occasions when you will write narratives or persuasive pieces. Most of these assignments will be in essay form. Your instructor will want to see a powerful, driving thesis statement in the introductory paragraphs of these assignments.

Do not make your thesis statement take in too much—this will make it too broad. On the other hand, do not make your thesis statement a single detail—then it will be too narrow. Think about an effective thesis in this way: If someone handed me this sentence, would I be able to use it to start writing because I would know the direction to take?

Characteristics of a Good Thesis Statement

1. reveals the issue or topic to be discussed

2. reveals a clear point of view

3. reveals a particular focus on the issue or topic to be discussed

4. usually shows the direction of the discussion (rhetorical point of view—contrast, compare, define, classify, and so forth)

Exercise 2:   *Group Activity: Writing Thesis Statements*

Form a group of three to five people. Write thesis statements together for each of the following topics. After you have finished, you will then exchange your set of thesis statements with another group. You will decide if the other group's thesis statements are effective. Be prepared to explain your answers.

1. professional women's hockey

2. buying shoes

3. exploiting animals

4. preparing a special meal for a festival

5. buying school supplies

6. volunteering your time

7. fixing a plugged sink

Exercise 3:   Deciding the Effectiveness of Thesis Statements

Work in pairs to decide if each sentence would be an effective thesis statement in an essay. In the spaces provided, write "too broad," "too narrow," "too vague," or "effective." Also write a comment on how you think the writer would handle the topic based on the thesis statement. Be prepared to defend and share your answers.

1. Children can be taught to share.

_____

_____

2. Young marriages never work.

_____

_____

3. Some games are just plain dumb.

_____

_____

4. Fresh herbs can make a meal.

_____

_____

5. Caring for elders has changed over the past 50 years in Canada.

_____

_____

6. Dogs have personalities.

_____

_____

7. Watching television is a waste of time.

_____

_____

8. Good discussion includes analysis, listening, commitment, and humour.

_____

_____

9. Groceries are too expensive, and rents are too high in this city.

_____

_____

10. Keeping exotic pets is a crime.

_____

_____

Writing the Introduction

Various ways of starting an introductory paragraph of an essay are given here. You may choose the one that seems to best serve your purposes or style. Do not try to use all of them because each is meant to do the same thing—kick-start the essay.

The introduction has three plain purposes: to get the reader interested in the topic; to provide some background information for the reader; to provide the thesis statement for the whole essay. The introduction should be at least five sentences long. If it is too short, it will not fulfill the three purposes. However, the introduction should not be lengthy, either, because you might disengage your reader. Since most academic writing you will do will be for courses, do not make your instructor or professor wade through a cluttered introduction.

Approaches to Getting the Reader Interested and Providing Background

1. *Head-On*

   Use an approach that tackles the issue in a direct and somewhat startling way. For example, suppose that you were writing about AIDS. If you were going to use a head-on approach, your introductory paragraph might look like this:

   > AIDS—today the word makes people stop and listen. Only about a decade ago, AIDS was a small concern to a handful of people. Most Canadians thought little about the topic and never dreamed it would someday touch their lives. But AIDS is multiplying at a terrifying rate; as much as a 67% increase has been noted by the medical community in Canada during the last two years. AIDS could become a modern-day epidemic, and everyone should know about the risks, the effects, and the prevention.

   Notice the first statement: It gets your attention. The last statement of the introductory paragraph is the thesis.

2. *Quotation*

   Your opening statement can be an effective quotation from a newspaper, a magazine, or a TV or radio program. Suppose that your essay was going to be about the high cost of living in 2005. Your introductory paragraph might look like this:

"Forty-three percent of Canadians are living below the poverty line. Many children are going to bed hungry and families are breaking up over money stress," claims Doreen Saunders, a member of the Canadian Coalition Against Poverty in a speech given to public educators on November 8, 2005, in Red Deer, Alberta. Further she says, "If someone with some power doesn't try to intervene in the process, our social services systems will become so inadequate that street families will become as common as those in Third World countries." Few Canadians would admit that Canada has a problem in this regard. However, the high cost of living in most Canadian cities is beginning to have devastating effects.

The first statements are direct quotations: The person is an expert, and her comments come from experience and knowledge. The last statement is the thesis statement.

3. *Personal Experience or Anecdote*

You can begin your essay by relating something that happened to you that bears on the topic. It could have been a critical event in your life, or it could have been something that seemed hardly noticeable at the time. Read the example below:

We were going to a family fun fair put on by a local community group, and I was feeling rather confused about taking my little boy and going with this new person in our lives. The place was very stuffy, crowded, and noisy, and my son was behaving like a brat because all of the excitement was overwhelming him. Just when I thought the whole idea and day had been a disaster, I noticed him in a quiet corner of a stairwell with my son. He was talking to my little boy calmly and at the same time was doing up the little guy's shoelaces. It was at that moment that I realized I loved those two people deeply. The love for someone is not the glamorous, wildly romantic notions shown in movies or magazines; instead it is peaceful and made up of small, almost invisible things.

The personal anecdote sets the tone of the essay—it shows a tender, compassionate side of the topic. The last statement is the thesis statement.

4. *Question*

Sometimes beginning an essay with a question or a series of questions can startle a reader into reading further. The writer must be prepared to answer the question in the introduction; otherwise, the question or questions become a cheap rhetorical trick. Look over the introduction below:

How can anyone survive on just fruits, vegetables, and grains? Isn't a person going to end up being malnourished on such a diet? People can and do exist well on such diets, and vegetarianism is perhaps one of the most misunderstood styles of eating. Prejudices exist against vegetarianism in North America, yet it has proven to be a far more healthful diet than any other.

The questions are answered. The last statement is the thesis statement.

5. *Engaging Fact or Statistic*

You can begin with any interesting statistic or fact that relates to your topic. Be sure to cite your source (show where you got your information).

Here are some examples:

According to one parenting group, 70% of birth control methods do not work! (PHT, 2004).

One out of three marriages ends in separation or divorce (StatsCan, 2003).

According to Wilfred J. Mudpie, pigs make the best pets!

Eighty-three percent of accidents happen in the home (Canada Safety Council, 2005).

According to a study completed by the University of Western Canada, men make up to one-third times more money than women for the same job (2005).

Start the essay with a shocking fact or statistic, then move the reader on to some background information. Place the thesis statement at the end of the introduction.

6. *Definition*

You may open your essay with a definition that runs one or more sentences long. Your thesis statement would then capture the main ideas of your definition. Be careful when you open using a definition. You do not want to reveal everything you will be saying in your essay in the introduction. It can become boring for the reader. In other words, do not tell everything through your definition. Here is an example:

Being a writer is seen by some as exciting and rewarding. Others say being a writer is being a famous person, one who is always in the spotlight. Some may even say that being a writer is like being a popular wit who is invited to every party and is the "talk of the town." However, being a writer is for the most part not any of these things. Instead, being a writer is a lonely, heartbreaking profession full of doubts and shadows.

The first statements are different definitions or conceptions of being a writer. The thesis is the last statement and provides a contrasting definition.

You may also divide the topic into parts and define each. Following is an example:

Vancouver is an important port on the west coast of Canada. It is a prominent place of industry and trade. Vancouver is a city of parks and gardens. In the day, Vancouver is a metropolis busy with commerce and the comings and goings of people. At night, it transforms itself into a centre for fun, food, and entertainment. Vancouver is a city of many faces.

The thesis is the last statement.

You can see then that the introduction can be handled in various ways. Try using one of these openers, then fill in some background for your reader, and finally give the reader the thesis statement. A thesis statement may be placed anywhere in the introductory paragraph, but most instructors prefer to see the thesis statement at the end of the introductory paragraph.

After you have formed a good working thesis and have some idea of what you want to include in the body paragraphs, go ahead and write a first draft of your essay. The next section provides some information about writing the body of support in an essay.

Exercise 4:   *Writing Clear Introductions*

Work in pairs. Write an introductory paragraph for three of the following topics. Use a different way of opening each introduction each time. Place your thesis statement at the end of the introduction. Be prepared to share your introductions.

1. mountain climbing

2. part-time work

3. fitness

4. bargains

5. good books

6. losing

7. winning

8. cell phones

9. travel

10. dieting

The Body of the Essay

When you write essays, you try to convince your reader of a few things. First, you want to show the reader that you have thought ideas through and given quite a bit of consideration to your topic. Further, you must provide examples or pieces of evidence that support the topic and are convincing.

Choosing Evidence

Choose good evidence by selecting powerful examples. Think of at least two reasons why the point you are trying to make could be true. Three reasons are even better. You must think of or find several real examples or illustrations or facts to support the point you are trying to establish.

Find examples or quotations to add weight to your argument. Keep the point you are trying to establish separate from the proof. Do not mix them in the same sentence.

Example:

In *Breaking Smith's Quarter Horse* by Paul St. Pierre, Smith is a man who may be too independent for his own good. He goes off to rescue some cattle in bad weather without letting anyone know where he is going.

The point: Smith may be too independent for his own good.

First piece of evidence to support the point: He goes off to rescue some cattle in bad weather without letting anyone know where he is going.

Choose evidence that is the most convincing you can find or think of. A weak example does not convince anyone.

Be confident in your statements. Say things like, "Mr. B. was a selfish character in the story who caused the ruin of several important people in his life." You may use a quotation like, "Mr. B. knew no one else by name, paid little attention to what others told him and considered his own career as the most significant in the firm." The first sentence sets out the point—the character was selfish. The second sentence provides proof that the first statement has merit.

Characteristics of the Body of Support

- Clearly laid out.
- Points clearly established.
- Points supported by strong examples, reasons, or facts—good evidence.
- Convincing through its well–thought-out organization.
- Concise and specific examples.

Using Transitions

Transitions are words that help bridge ideas. In the previous chapter on paragraphs, you will see lists of transitions that work for different purposes and in different rhetorical modes or patterns of organization.

Use transitions between major points. Use transitional sentences between body paragraphs. Transitions keep the flow in writing.

The Conclusion

The last paragraph of your essay is called a concluding paragraph or a conclusion. Your concluding paragraph may provide three things for the reader:

1. In a longer essay or research paper, it should restate the thesis. Write the thesis again, but use different words.
2. It should highlight the main points of the essay. Look at each body paragraph and summarize each in a few words. In a short essay, summarizing main points may not be as important as in a long paper. Ask your instructor or professor about preferences.

3. The conclusion should leave the reader with a general thought on the topic. Instead of simply summing up your ideas and leaving the reader there, add a worldly thought on the topic. This general thought provides closure in the reader's mind.

Note, however, that the conclusion is not the place to introduce new ideas or points that you have not mentioned previously in the essay. Instead, the last paragraph is the closing stage of a presentation—a place where you tie off the ideas and then impress the reader. You want to leave the reader thinking about what you have said.

As you write, it is important to learn to read other writers' works as a writer would read. Begin to learn to examine much more than the content of writing. Begin to look for the style and the structure of what you read. Writers learn to write from reading other writers. You will, too.

Writing the First Draft

After you have developed your ideas and evidence and composed your thesis statement, develop a sketch outline. Fill in the topic sentences, major ideas, points, and evidence. Think about your opening sentence. Then begin to write your first draft.

Allow yourself to compose. Write ideas as they occur to you and do not worry about correcting all the mistakes. Editing out errors is part of the polishing of the piece. It has no place at the beginning of the writing process.

As Henriette Anne Klauser suggests in *Writing on Both Sides of the Brain: Breakthrough Techniques in Writing*:

> When you edit and write at the same time, the result is often a disaster: a disaster for you as a writer and eventually for your reader. Purple patches come from the unrestricted pen. Go back and edit later. Later is when you invite the logical sequential strength side of you to come forward and apply all the techniques of good grammar and construction that have been drilled into you since the beginning of your school days (15).

Peer Editing

Many instructors use a technique called peer editing in their classes. Peer editing means another student from your class is going to read your paper and comment on it. You will do the same. Peer editing can be very useful, particularly if everyone is committed to the task, and the criteria for evaluation are clear. Criteria are often embedded in checklists.

Review the following three peer editing checklists. The first checklist helps you to focus on organization and evidence—the content—in essays. The second concentrates on grammar and mechanics features of the writing. The last checklist centres on writing style.

Peer Editing Sheet 1:   *Organization and Evidence*

Writer's name: _____ Editor's name: _____ Date:_____

Read the piece of writing, paying attention to organizational structures and development features. You will read for grammar, usage, spelling, and punctuation errors using a different editing sheet. Check the appropriate spaces. Be prepared to provide reasons for your answers.

Introductory Paragraph:

Begins with an effective "grabber"   yes _____   no _____
Provides one–two background sentences   yes _____   no _____
Thesis statement: end of introduction   yes _____   no _____
Thesis statement: clear, directing   yes _____   no _____
Rhetorical mode of the thesis statement: _____

Body Paragraph 1:

Begins with a clear topic sentence   yes _____   no _____
Provides three main points   yes _____   no _____
Provides specific support for points   yes _____   no _____
Provides transitional sentence to next paragraph   yes _____   no _____

Body Paragraph 2:

Begins with a clear topic sentence   yes _____   no _____
Provides three main points   yes _____   no _____
Provides specific support for points   yes _____   no _____
Provides transitional sentence to next paragraph   yes _____   no _____

Body Paragraph 3 (4, 5+):

Begins with a clear topic sentence   yes _____   no _____
Provides three main points   yes _____   no _____
Provides specific support for points   yes _____   no _____
Provides transitional sentence to next paragraph   yes _____   no _____

Concluding Paragraph:

Restates the thesis   yes _____   no _____
Sums up main ideas   yes _____   no _____
Last sentence effectively wraps up discussion   yes _____   no _____

Comments: (Name one thing you liked and one thing you didn't like about the piece.)

_____

_____

_____

Peer Editing Sheet 2:   *Grammar, Mechanics, and Spelling*

Writer's name: _____ Editor's name: _____ Date:_____

Read the piece of writing, paying attention to grammar, spelling, usage, and punctuation.

Check the appropriate spaces.

Types of errors A problem?

Grammar:

Subject-verb agreement errors	yes _____	no _____
Misplaced or dangling modifiers	yes _____	no _____
Comma splices	yes _____	no _____
Fragments	yes _____	no _____
Run-on sentences	yes _____	no _____

Punctuation:

Comma use	yes _____	no _____
Semi-colon use	yes _____	no _____
Colon use	yes _____	no _____
Apostrophe use	yes _____	no _____

Other Features:

Point of view shifts	yes _____	no _____
Pronoun agreement errors	yes _____	no _____
Sentence logic problems	yes _____	no _____
Verb tense shift errors	yes _____	no _____
Spelling Problems:	yes _____	no _____

Comments: (Name one thing you liked and one thing you disliked about the editing of this paper.)

_____

_____

_____

_____

_____

_____

Peer Editing Sheet 3: *Reviewing Writer's Style*

Writer's name: _____ Editor's name: _____ Date:_____

Read the piece of writing with the intent of looking at the writer's style: how the writer says something. Check the appropriate spaces.

<u>**Style Feature**</u>	<u>**Effective?**</u>	
Sentences:		
Sentence variety (different patterns)	yes _____	no _____
Variety in sentence length	yes _____	no _____
Words:		
Appropriate selection	yes _____	no _____
Good use of adverbs	yes _____	no _____
Concise words chosen	yes _____	no _____
Effective diction	yes _____	no _____
Punctuation:		
Interesting variety	yes _____	no _____
Effective	yes _____	no _____
Tone:		
Writer's tone is appropriate	yes _____	no _____
Audience:		
The intended audience seems clear	yes _____	no _____
Tone and audience seem to fit together	yes _____	no _____

Comments: (Name one thing you liked about this writer's style. Name one thing you did not like. Add a recommendation to help the writer improve his or her style.)

_____

_____

_____

_____

_____

_____

Assignment

In-class writing: Write a short essay (500 words) on one of three topics the instructor provides. You will have one hour to write. Use five minutes to generate ideas. Use five minutes to make a sketch outline. Write for 35 minutes. Leave 15 minutes for editing. Double space your work.

Bonus Exercise: *Avoiding Sexist Language*

Sexism in language use has to do with favouring one gender's point of view over another. If one point of view is the only one presented, then readers and writers may think that it represents all points of view. Use the third person plural point of view to eliminate sexism. The Internet provides some interesting information about sexism in language. Visit sites connected to college and university libraries and writing centres for quality information and examples.

Rewrite each sentence, eliminating sexism:

1. Every man wants the freedom to find happiness for himself.

2. Most of the time, corporations try to find the best man for the job.

3. Everyone decided to vote with his own conscience.

4. Everybody should do what she can to help.

5. The reporters were trying to find out who was responsible and if he was available for comment.

CHECKOUT

Here are some of the ideas you will take away with you after you have completed the chapter:

1. The writing preferences of individual instructors may vary.

2. Conventionally, an academic essay has three parts.

3. A thesis statement is a sentence that states the main idea of an essay.

4. Most student writing assignments require expository writing.

5. Peer editing checklists can improve your editing and writing skills.

chapter 5

Writing Narrative Essays

Chapter Objectives

What will you have learned when you have completed this chapter?

You will be able to

1. prepare for writing a narrative essay through recall and reflection.

2. choose, then put into words, an appropriate writing tone.

3. identify the point of view you've established in your essay.

4. consider the role played by your writer's voice.

Introduction

Narrative essays are pieces of writing that relate experience or an observation. They may tell a story, but their main purpose is not storytelling. Instead, they explore experience and reflect on it. As a writer, you want to do something more with your experience than simply tell about it. For example, you may have experienced a life-threatening accident in your life. Just to narrate what the experience was like is probably not enough. In some way, you want to use the experience as a tool to understanding a value, idea, belief, or assumption you have. Perhaps the experience helped you explore your faith or your belief in what it means to be human. This chapter will introduce you to some of the ideas connected to narrative essays and will provide strategies to make narrative essay writing more than storytelling.

Narrative Essays: Finding Relational Elements

Stories are part of the human journey through life. Our experiences shape us and help to make us the individuals we are. In academic writing, stories are called narratives. Narrative essays go beyond mere storytelling: They are meant to help us make connections and enrich our learning lives. The following section will provide you with a general introduction to the genre called narrative essays.

Purpose

You have probably been moved by someone's story. Maybe it was a story told by a mother who had lost a child in war or a story told about a person's remarkable courage or struggle. These types of stories inspire us in many ways.

Most of the time, however, writers have a larger purpose than just relating a story. They may wish to educate, shock, persuade, entertain, or motivate their readers. All of these purposes are equally valid. Using narrative as a tool to achieve your purpose in writing is a good strategy because most readers respond positively to stories. Although changing readers' perspectives is not an easy task, it remains one of the noble goals of great works of literature.

As you write your narrative, think about what point it is you are trying to make. Why are you telling the story to your reader? In order to answer the question, you must do some personal reflection about the incident. In other words, you will have to think about the incident in a deeper way than you have done before.

Reflection is the process of recalling, reacting to, and evaluating experience or observation. Often reflection considers your prior understanding of an experience and compares it to a new understanding. From the process, you may develop a new plan of action and new knowledge. Dr. David Boud, a renowned professor of adult, higher, and professional education from the University of Technology in Sydney, Australia, has characterized reflection as "turning experience into learning." He believes people can "animate learning" by working with their experiences.

RECALLING To begin reflection, concentrate on a particular experience you have had in your life or on an observation or set of observations you may have made. Take a few minutes to focus.

- In a few sentences, relate the experience you have had.
- Note who was involved.
- Note the particular place the event occurred.
- Note the specific situation.
- Note any specific details you can recall.
- Reread what you have written. Does it recall the experience fairly accurately as far as you can remember? If so, you are ready to react to what you have recalled.

REACT AND EVALUATE Use these questions to help you begin to recall your reactions to the experience and possibly to react to and evaluate them in new or different ways. Write down your answers as completely as you can. Work in a quiet, private space as you gather your recollections, reactions, and evaluation.

Questions to Assist Reflection

1. How did you react to the people in the experience at the time?

2. How did you react to the situation at the time?

3. What feelings about the experience do you recall?

4. What challenged you in the experience?

5. What surprised you in the experience?

6. Did the experience challenge a personal value?

7. Are your feelings about the experience different now? How?

8. What do you think you learned from the experience?

Now review what you have written in response to the above questions. Have any of your answers surprised you? What is unexpected about them?

Point of View, Voice, and Tone

Most of the time, narrative essays are written from a personal point of view. Some narratives can use a third person perspective, but generally speaking, you will use a first person view since the essay centres on you and your experience. The "I" point of view invites your reader into a more intimate discussion.

Developing your own voice in writing can include a number of elements. The writer's voice means you can "hear" the personality of the writer because it comes through the writing to the reader. Here are some key elements that work to create your writer's voice:

- You reveal something about your personality in your writing.
- You demonstrate you are aware of your audience (reader).
- You create an interaction with your reader: Your reader or audience matters to you.
- You are committed to your topic: The subject matters to you.
- You attempt to bring the topic to life: You try to make the writing lively and interesting in your own way.
- You work to hold your reader's attention.

You will recall that tone in writing has to do with your attitude towards your subject or your readers. You may choose a formal or informal tone that expresses anger, joy, sadness, optimism, pessimism, humour, or gravity. Your tone may be ironic or satirical. At the same time, your tone is conveyed by your word choice or diction. If you choose words that generally have a positive connotation, then your tone will be more upbeat. The words you choose should support your attitude to your subject.

Whatever tone you select, it must be appropriate. Consider your audience, your subject, and your own voice when you are deciding the tone to use. Inappropriate tone will cause your narrative essay to falter. You may alienate or put off your reader by being insensitive in tone.

Adding Description

Your narrative should contain some description. You will be recounting what happened or what you observed, and you must try to make it interesting to read. Choosing precise words will add liveliness to your description and to the narrative essay overall. Choose appropriate diction. For example, if your tone is serious, choose words that convey a serious tone.

Hints for Description

- Use adverbs.
- Avoid clichés and tired expressions.
- Add meaning and detail, not just empty words.
- Use specific details.
- Vary sentence patterns.
- Vary punctuation.
- Use concise verbs.

Examples:

Narrative Passage without Much Description

> After I purchased the playpen from the store, I took it to the parking lot and put it into the trunk of my car. I did not notice the car beside me at the time. As I got into my car and prepared to back out, I was slammed from behind by the car beside me as the driver manoeuvred it out of its space.

Narrative Passage with Description

> As an expectant mother anticipating her first baby, I felt exhilarated after purchasing the Playmore Playpen from my local Sears store. Joyfully and lovingly, I packed it into the trunk of my old Toyota Celica waiting in the mall's parking lot, and in my excitement, I took little notice of the vehicle parked beside me on my right. Happily, I squeezed into the driver's seat and prepared to leave. Suddenly my whole body was slammed forward into the steering column! The driver of the Ford truck parked on my right had crashed into the back of my car as he abruptly manoeuvred out of his parking space.

Clearly, the second passage gives the reader more information while the writer's tone and voice are more evident. The reader may have more sympathy for the writer in the second passage because of the additional information.

Transformative Experience and Narratives

Transformative experience has traditionally referred to experiences connected to conversion, enlightenment, or salvation, but many incidents in life can change people deeply and dramatically. These experiences happen over time and produce enormous change in the way people think about and live their lives.

There is an element of discovery, sometimes even personal truth, gained by a transformative experience. For example, students who come from a small place or a different culture to a large urban university feel the impact of the new setting, the unfamiliarity of the discourses within various communities, and the divergent belief structures found within the university and surrounding populations. At first, the experience may simply feel strange to them, but over the course of several semesters, students begin to experience changes in their own ways of behaving, maybe even in their own values. They may discover new truths about themselves, too. Unexpected or unplanned-for experiences can cause change as well.

Traumatic incidents can also change people. Having a life-threatening illness or disease transforms how people see and know themselves. Moreover, terrible accidents or bearing witness to horrifying events can be transformative experiences because people are forever changed by them. However, smaller but poignant events also produce remarkable effects. The birth of a child, a marriage, a personal triumph like winning a race, a conversation, a job, or a new relationship all have the potential to be transformative. Broadly speaking, transformative experiences include reflection.

Sample Narratives

Exercise 1:   *Reading and Responding to Narratives*

Work in a group of three to five people. Choose one of the selections from the narratives below. Read the narrative and then use the questions for discussion to get conversation going in your group. Write your answers in note form on a large sheet of paper or on Microsoft Powerpoint. Be prepared to post your answers for the rest of the class to see.

The Love of My Vehicular Life Will Always Be a '71 VW Bug

by Linda Fulkerson

Linda Fulkerson touches on the North American love of the automobile, but she also connects owning a car, driving, personal meaning, and relationships.

I drive a 1996 Mazda pickup—it has provided me with years of reliable service and I hope that it will provide me with many more. Yet despite this longstanding relationship, when it passes on, it will be remembered as a good vehicle, nothing more. It will pull no heart strings and the replacement decision will be purely intellectual.

What makes a car special is not the car itself, but rather the experiences that surround it. For that reason, the love of my vehicular life will always be my 1971 Volkswagen Bug.

In my late teens, my parents gave me a gift of cash. My mother insisted that her gift be used towards university; my father put no restrictions on his and we decided that I would acquire my first car. I wanted a VW Bug for two reasons; firstly, they were cute, and secondly, I knew my Dad had a weakness for them, and would help me car shop.

And help he did, lecturing me to buy a regular Bug, not the Superbeetle with the larger engine. Imagine his shock on discovering that the car we purchased was indeed a Superbeetle, the distinctive longer 'nose' not being found in the first year's model. However, this was now overlooked, and Dad set out to teach me to drive a standard. We spent many hours circling an industrial park.

She (for somehow I knew the car was feminine) was not a thing of beauty. She was pale blue and eventually sported an orange replacement fender as a result of a minor accident.

One visit with my father led us to a brilliant idea; we should sand and prime the rust spots to lengthen her serviceable years. After we finished the sanding Dad presented me with a spray can of primer. As I began systematically spraying the sanded spots Dad told me that he had a second can and would start at the other end. I was dismayed, upon moving to the back of the car, to discover Dad was using white primer. Thus began my period of owning a multi-hued Bug.

The Bug's spirit finally gave out one day on the way to visit Dad. She was towed back to my home in Mission where her fate was debated. It was decided to repair her mechanically and then restore her to a glory that I had never seen. A rebuilt engine restored her spirit and a five-month long beauty treatment, complete with new hood, fenders, slipcovers and a Porsche Red paint job gave her a beauty that turned heads. Dad helped with the financing. In all I owned my Bug for 17 years. I finally decided I needed a vehicle that had a working heater that could keep the inside of the car windows frost-free.

Even now, a glimpse of an older Beetle brings a wave of nostalgia. Those times spent with my father somehow don't seem that distant. I still have a longing to own another Beetle, but realize that it is just a desire to recapture memories. Like the car, my father has passed from my life, though our relationship continued for eight years after selling my Bug. I will never have another car like her, because I will never know another man like my father.

Source: Linda Fulkerson, "The Love of My Vehicular Life Will Always Be a '71 VW Bug," Vancouver Sun 5 *August 2005: D9. Reprinted by permission of Linda Fulkerson.*

Discussion Questions:

What specifically does she say about her transformative experience? What tone does Linda Fulkerson use? Is it appropriate? What did you notice about her diction? Can you characterize the writer's voice? What do you think the writer learned? From what point of view does she write? Have you had a transformative experience that relates to the joy of owning or driving a car?

A Summer Student Experience

by Andrea Pouteaux

Read the following selection. Andrea Pouteaux has been unexpectedly transformed by her summer work experience as a student.

When school started this year, I asked all of my colleagues, "What did you do for the summer?" I received the typical responses: waitress, cashier, lifeguard, took classes, or nothing! When they asked the question in return, I told them I worked for a research team called the Southern Saskatchewan Urban Aboriginal Health Coalition. My work included reviewing transcripts taken at seven different sharing circles from one Métis and one First Nations community, developing and distributing a communiqué to the communities, attending groups and advisory committee meetings, and working with the research team to put together a proposal for the Canadian Institutes of Health Research to acquire more funding to continue research with the two communities to explore the area of culturally respectful care. It sure was not the typical response they were anticipating. I was proud to say what I did this summer.

What did I observe?

My job as an undergraduate research assistant allowed me to observe. I could be compared to a sponge, soaking in all the information I could until, by the end of the summer, I was completely saturated. I was able to observe and participate in mature research group meetings. It was impressive to see how the group could communicate in such a wide variety of ways; via telephone, e-mail, teleconferences and meetings, yet information was efficiently and effectively exchanged and shared every time. I watched the team adapt to new communication methods because the group was quite large, and team members lived in different cities.

I also watched how the group respected one another's opinions. If there was a suggestion made, only positive things were said about it. No one made anyone else feel intimidated. Every idea on how to work with these communities was considered and valued. This openness to new ideas is what kept this group together and functioning.

During my time this summer, I saw how committed this group was to the research they were involved in, but more importantly, I saw their commitment to the two communities, Standing Buffalo First Nation and Regina Métis Sport and Culture. The research team was in it for the common good of the two communities. I saw how selfless they were in giving up their time, ideas and putting all of themselves into this research as if it were their only passion in life.

What did I learn?

All of the learning had to be turned into something. I realized that all of my observing turned into a great learning experience. I learned about my own cultural background. I am Métis and did not know about the beliefs and values my ancestors had. It was enlightening to read the transcripts taken at the sharing circles to see what is important to these communities and what aspects of their culture they would like to see carried out in the hospital setting. I felt like I was reading a chapter from my past and felt extremely enriched and privileged to be given the opportunity to read the transcripts and be able to benefit personally from them.

I learned how to communicate in a group. I have always been a one-on-one communicator, but I quickly had to learn how to communicate the same message to several group members. I can safely say that it is not an easy task; sometimes information is misunderstood, sometimes the e-mail does not arrive safely, but it was great to learn how to exchange information throughout a large group.

Not only did I learn how to communicate to the research group, but I had the chance to send out a communiqué to much larger groups, the two communities we were working with. I helped construct and put together a communiqué that was sent to Standing Buffalo First Nation and Regina Métis Sport and Culture to keep them updated on the research. We wanted to encourage them and let them know that we had not forgotten about them as a team. The feedback we received from the communiqué was phenomenal and the communities could not have been more thrilled to receive feedback from the team.

The only reason I had a job this summer was because of the wonderful openness of the two communities. If they were not willing and gracious enough to share their thoughts and feelings, our research group would not have been such a success. From the honest and sincere transcripts, I was given the chance to do a transcript analysis on the seven transcripts. I picked out line by line the themes that recurred throughout the dialogue. It was a tedious process, but in the end, we found commonalities between the very unique communities.

How did it change me?

As I look back at my summer opportunity, I can only see growth in myself. I feel as though I have been rewarded with the knowledge I have taken away from this experience. I have learned about culturally respectful care, a phrase that did not mean nearly as much to me three months ago as it does now. I can not help but smile when I think about how I am one step ahead of my colleagues because of the opportunity I have had. I know I will be a culturally respectful nurse when I do graduate from the NEPS program. When I am working on a ward in the near future, I hope I can be an example to others as they watch me give care that is respectful and equal across cultures.

Thank you to IPHRC for funding my job this summer as an undergraduate research assistant working with the Southern Saskatchewan Urban Aboriginal Health Coalition under the caring supervision of Dr. Marlene Smadu. I truly appreciate the opportunity and have observed, learned, and have become a more respectful future nurse.

Source: Andrea Pouteaux, "A Summer Student Experience," The Aboriginal Nurse, *Winter 2004: 9. Reprinted with permission.*

Discussion Questions:

What specifically was her transformative experience? What did the writer learn? What is the tone she uses? Can you characterize the writer's voice? From what point of view does the writer write?

Steaks, Sticks, and Smoke

by Paul Rush

Read the following selection. Paul Rush describes a common experience of cooking outdoors, but he personalizes the event.

We all want to have a spacious deck. And on that deck a capacious barbecue. And on that barbecue, a delicious feast. And that's where I have problems. I have decks and I have a couple of old but adequate charcoal barbecues. But somehow I don't come up with those delicious feasts. In fact, most of what I cook tends to be dry and chewy rather than moist and succulent. My barbecue bungling goes back a long way. Many years ago, I had a small tabletop barbecue. When guests came over for dinner one Sunday, I set out a supply of beer and four thin steaks. Then I started the barbecue—and my troubles as well. I had no charcoal starter, so I lit a fire with twigs. When I dug into my charcoal bag, I found only eight briquettes. Even I knew this was a weak fuel supply, so I threw on more twigs and lit the charcoal by blowing on each piece. After that, I applied faulty reasoning.

My fear was that if I waited until the briquettes were ready, when they're covered with fine, white ash, they would burn out before the steaks were done. So as soon as all the charcoal was started, I tossed on the steaks. No, they didn't sizzle. Then we all had a few beer. A half-hour later, the bottoms of the steaks had changed from red to light brown and some of the charcoal had gone out. I relit it and threw on more twigs. We all had a few more beer.

About two hours later, I pulled the steaks off the grill, still pale brown on the outside and grey in the middle and dry as a Prairie summer. I can't remember if we ate them, but I am sure that we all had a few beer.

I did get somewhat better at barbecuing, but I never cooked anything fancy and I always seemed to be operating in the midst of a cloud of smoke and flame. Once when I hosted an impromptu gathering on a Sunday, I started up the barbecue (not waiting for the white ash stage; I was a little low on fuel again) and threw on a mess of fatty burgers. There was so much smoke and flame that a distinguished university professor and a Venezuelan social worker offered to take over.

"Too much flame, Paul," they shouted over the sizzle. "Spray water on it." "Are you crazy?" I said. "It took me a long time to get this charcoal going."

I couldn't refuse (and, besides, my eyes stung from the smoke), so I let them take control. But in my heart I love the smoke and flame that spews from my barbecue, and when, on rare occasions, I barbecue for myself, I cook lamb chops. Let the charcoal almost get to the white ash stage. Put on the lamb chops and let the droplets of fat start a major fire. Put the top back on and put out the flame. Take the top off and stand back from the conflagration. Turn the chops with a big fork and repeat the process. The result? Perfect chops, crisp and blackened on the outside, pink and (dare I say it?) succulent inside. Although they are not something you would wish to serve to company.

I think my troubles with barbecues are buried deep in my childhood. I go back to the days before barbecues, when those who liked charred food tended to cook over campfires. The easiest meal was a hot dog on a sharp stick. If you wanted fancy, you opened a can of beans and dumped the contents into a pot wedged into the flames. If, for some reason, you wanted steak, I suppose you cooked one on a stick. An asbestos glove was also useful, not only for handling the pots and pans, but for plucking potatoes out of the ash. For dessert, you had flaming marshmallows.

It was a simpler time in which one ate a great deal of ash and a few wood chips, and the food was at once burnt and raw. It set me on the path where you'll still find me today if you sneak up on me at the barbecue: smoke rising, flames spewing, hot fat popping and hamburgers sliding through the grill down into the coals.

Not pretty, but it's home to me.

Source: Paul Rush, "Steaks, Sticks, and Smoke," Canadian Home Workshop, *Apr. 2005: 82.*

Discussion Questions:

How has the experience transformed the writer, do you think? What has Paul Rush learned? What tone does the writer use? Is it appropriate? How? What did you notice about the writer's diction? How would you characterize the writer's voice? Can you think of a childhood experience that has been transformative for you?

Bonus Exercise: *Infinitives and Negatives*

An infinitive is a verbal (a word that has been formed from a verb). It consists of the base form of a verb and the word "to."

Examples of Infinitives:

- to whisper

- to lock

- to prepare

Infinitive phrases include objects.

Examples of Infinitive Phrases:

- to whisper a secret

- to lock the window

- to prepare the evening meal

Infinitives can have a variety of functions in sentences. Sometimes they can be the subjects of sentences. At other times, they can serve as objects (direct or indirect) of the verb.

Examples of Functions of Infinitive Phrases:

To whisper a secret is considered rude. (infinitive phrase as subject)

Felicity advised us to lock the window. (infinitive phrase as indirect object)

At times, you may want to make the infinitive phrase negative. In that case, do not split the infinitive with the word "not."

Example:

Felicity advised us to *not* lock the window. (Incorrect. "Not" split the infinitive phrase.)

Felicity advised us not to lock the window. (Correct. The infinitive phrase has not been split by "not.")

In the following sentences, insert the word "not" to make each of the infinitive phrases negative. Do not split the infinitives with "not."

1. Mrs. Truggles began to sing loudly.

2. To discuss the problem with Antonio would be the best solution.

3. To steal the ancient jewels from the museum in Cairo was the gang's obsession.

4. Mr. Rigali and his son decided to open a bicycle shop in the downtown core.

5. To wrap the cheese in brown paper will help the curing process.

Assignment

Write a narrative essay of 700 words, using the format given below.

1. Choose an experience from your life that you consider transformative.
2. In the first one or two body paragraphs, describe the experience. Use the tips given previously for descriptive writing.
3. In the second part of the body of the essay, discuss how the experience transformed you. Use some techniques relating to reflection provided earlier in the chapter. Consider: Have your values changed? Have your attitudes changed? Be specific. Use description as well.
4. In the final paragraph of your essay, discuss what you learned. Think more globally in this section. Try to think of the "big picture" rather than stating the obvious. Try to come up with how the transformative experience helped you learn or became a deeper personal truth for you.

CHECKOUT

Here are some of the ideas you will take away with you after you have completed the chapter:

1. Narrative essay writing is more than just storytelling.

2. Choose precise descriptive words to catch your reader's interest.

3. The tone of your writing can win over your reader.

4. Careful editing of your writing shows respect for the reader.

chapter 6

Expository Writing

Chapter Objectives

What will you have learned when you have completed this chapter?

You will be able to

1. write an expository essay informing readers about an academic subject.

2. provide reasoned support for your opinions in an expository essay.

3. draw a timeline to help you in developing your thesis statement.

4. take advantage of rhetorical modes to shape ideas in expository writing.

5. benefit your writing by appropriate placement of transitional words and phrases.

Introduction

Expository writing informs readers. The writer may choose to write using opinions, but they must be reasoned out and supported. As a student, most of the writing you will do for courses will be expository. A nursing student may be asked to write an essay about nursing principles; a biology student may be asked to write an essay about ecosystems; a history student may be asked to write about the first administrator of British Columbia.

As a student using expository writing as the form of written expression most of the time, you will want to know about some of the rules and guidelines called the conventions of writing. In particular, this book will discuss the conventions of essay writing.

Common Rhetorical Modes in Expository Writing

Rhetoric is a term originally used by the ancient Romans and Greeks to refer to the powers of oration. The ancient Greek orators, known for their eloquent use of language, gave moving, persuasive speeches about important themes many centuries before text was available. To be a brilliant orator in those times meant a life of study of rhetoric, dialectics, and grammar. Today rhetoric has just as much to do with persuasive writing as with great speeches.

Rhetoric is the effective use of persuasive language. Some of the tools used in rhetoric to organize ideas are still valuable today. These tools, often referred to as rhetorical modes, develop ideas by arranging them into patterns: by time, definition, cause and effect, comparison and contrast, classification and division, and so forth. Rhetorical modes were discussed earlier, in Chapter 4, in looking at the organization of essays.

Expository writing also takes advantage of rhetorical modes to shape ideas in a variety of ways, depending on the writer's purpose. For example, if you wanted to write about childcare in Canada, you could organize your ideas with the use of different rhetorical modes: A historical view of childcare in Canada employs a time order or process approach. If you look for similarities and differences between traditional Aboriginal childcare and 18th century European, then you are using a comparison and contrast mode. If you want to consider the range of childcare in Canada in 2006, you might put the services into groupings; in other words, you would be using a classification approach. Should you wish to define what childcare is, then your approach would use a definition rhetorical mode.

Process Analysis

A process analysis is a piece of writing that describes something that happens over time. It is writing that deals with the stages of something or the sequence of events that take place in an activity of some sort. Process analysis writing is used a lot in many subject areas. For example, much writing within a course in one of the technologies will include how to do something: how to program a computer using a special new computer language, how to measure something, or how to design something. Many science courses and health courses also use the process pattern. In a nursing course, students might read how to change a dressing, how to give an injection, how to chart, or how to communicate with a worried patient. In chemistry, much of the writing within the texts and the writing done by students will involve some sort of process design or pattern. Your process pattern could be made up of:

- stages
- a sequence or set of sequences
- steps
- dates
- points of separation

To use a process pattern in an essay, a writer must have a very clear idea of the process, how it is arranged or how the writer wants to arrange it, and why the writer wants to talk about it in the first place. Remember that a thesis statement tries to convince. If a writer chooses to use the process pattern, she or he must let the reader know in the thesis statement the point of telling about the process in the first place. Is the writer trying to be interesting? Is he or she trying to compare one process with another? Is the writer trying to help the reader understand something by analyzing a process? Keep this in mind when you write an essay that is going to describe a process. There must be some angle of interest in the thesis statement; otherwise, the reader could simply look up the information in a reference book.

Examples:

1. Here's how I make my own clothes!

(Poor thesis statement. True, it shows process analysis. But there is no angle of interest. Why would anyone want to bother reading this?)

2. Any woman can make herself a dress that is glamorous and trendy yet relatively inexpensive compared to designer labels.

(Better: Now there is a point to writing the essay. The writer will talk about making a garment and show through the description of the process how the dress will save the maker money without sacrificing style.).

You may choose to employ a timeline, used for arranging stages over a duration. As you do your thinking or arranging, you will have some sort of framework in which to put your writing. The arrangement may be a sequence of events, so the events themselves can be charted out on a line. Not all events are clear when we try to describe something, so often we are forced to cluster smaller sets of events into stages. When we do this, we are categorizing ideas. We cluster small steps into larger stages, and we may then choose to chart these stages on a timeline.

Another advantage of drawing a timeline is that it can also help you to develop your thesis statement. For example, if you drew a timeline with four stages shown by four important dates in Canadian history, you might then develop the following thesis: *Canada has gone through four distinct stages during its journey from colony to independent nation.* After you have charted the sequence on the timeline and developed a good working thesis, you might start thinking about other keywords or phrases that you would want to include in your essay.

Key phrases help the reader follow the passage of time throughout the essay. You might choose actual dates to mark the time, but if you are simply putting forth phrases, you will probably use transitions like *next, later, after that, soon, by this time,* and so forth. (Refer to the detailed list of transitions in Chapter 3 for a more complete listing of process or time order transitions.) In addition, you may want to repeat key phrases in the process itself. This not only reminds the reader of your thesis, but also lets the reader know where in the overall process he or she is reading.

Comparison and Contrast

Throughout your life you have learned by comparing and contrasting how things are the same and how they are different. You might have discovered more about apartments by comparing them to houses; you might also have known which dogs on your street to pat and which ones to leave alone through the use of comparison/contrast.

The first stage of carrying out a comparison could not be more straightforward. Take two people, events, ideas, books, works of art, or two of anything, and ask yourself: "How are these two things the same? How different?" By so doing, you are conducting a comparative analysis.

A well-planned comparison/contrast essay will almost write itself, but its initial construction takes some thought. Deciding which two things to compare broadly is quite an easy task. But then you must decide how to compare them. A point of comparison is a characteristic that you choose that is common to both items being compared, and to be effective it must be clear and logical. For example, let's suppose you wanted to compare children living in Canada with children living in China. One point of comparison might be education because both groups of children attend school. Another point of comparison might be entertainment because children all over the world love to play. Finally, the last point of comparison you might choose is responsibility in the family. Most children are responsible for helping out the family to lesser or greater degrees.

It is unproductive and confusing to talk about points that do not relate in some way to the two broad categories you are writing about, and so well-thought-out points are critical to a good essay using a comparison/contrast pattern. Also remember that each point of comparison must be distinct; do not overlap these major points because your writing will become repetitious.

Here is a further example. Suppose you want to discuss Calgary and Vancouver in relation to one another because you want to determine which place to live. Perhaps you have decided on four points of comparison:

1. population
2. industry
3. climate
4. architecture

Thus you would not include harbours in your discussion because Calgary has none. If you added a point of comparison like annual rainfall, you would find it overlaps with climate. However, if you did decide to discuss Vancouver's harbour because you believed it to be a very important feature, then you might invent a point of comparison like transportation systems. Similarly, if annual rainfall seemed vital to your discussion, then you could include it in the discussion of climate.

Once you have thought out your points of comparison and sketched out a few notes for each or planned some of the discussion, then you must decide the actual structure of the comparison/contrast essay. Will you discuss each city separately? Will you use the points of comparison for each paragraph and include both cities under each point? The choice is yours. Try to imagine which one would work best. Sometimes it is good practice to include both cities in the discussion throughout the essay because the points of comparison become the feature of the paper. But at the same time this type of set-up can become rather tedious to read if the writer is not paying attention to style.

Model 1:

Introductory paragraph

Body paragraph 1: Calgary

- population

- industry

- climate

- architecture

Body paragraph 2: Vancouver

- population

- industry

- climate

- architecture

Concluding paragraph

Model 2:

Introductory paragraph

Body paragraph 1: population

- Calgary
- Vancouver

Body paragraph 2: industry

- Calgary
- Vancouver

Body paragraph 3: climate

- Calgary
- Vancouver

Body paragraph 4: architecture

- Calgary
- Vancouver

Concluding paragraph

Both of these models will work; however, each has different characteristics. As you can see, the first model will only contain two large body paragraphs; this essay would be awkward, and it would not really be a conventional essay because it does not fit the minimum number of body paragraphs. Besides that, it requires the reader to remember the points made in the first half of the essay in order to compare them to the information given in the second portion. Obviously, the longer the essay, the more difficult it becomes for the reader to hold pertinent ideas in mind. In the second model, points of comparison are arranged by paragraph so that they are emphasized and are easier for the reader to retain. Keywords to use in comparison/contrast essays are words like *similarly*, *same*, *different*, *on the other hand*, *conversely*, and so forth.

Most experts agree that comparing and contrasting are two of the most important of the critical skills. One composition professor observes just how relational this skill is: "I ask my students to think about people, places, and things, as well as ideas. I ask them to explore the connections between time and space, between global and local concerns, between divergent lifestyles and cultures, between events and ideas, between individualism and independence" (V. P. Stephen, "Hello, out there . . . Is anybody thinking?" *Teaching* Fall 2004: 54).

The following example shows how one student wrote about an important event in his life—whether to buy or to rent.

To Buy or to Rent?

Recently couples have been having a hard time deciding whether to own or rent a home. Because interest rates have risen, potential homeowners have had to weigh the benefits of owning against those of renting. This problem is even more confusing because of the high rents that are now being charged. In some aspects renting may seem securer, but owning has far more benefits.

First, the investment in land has always been the safest. A mortgage may seem like a large debt, but property value never decreases, and the opportunity of selling can mean receiving more money than has been paid. For example, homes in 2004 have increased in value by at least 150% since 1984. In fact, paying rent is paying someone else's mortgage, and receiving no investment or property in return. Also, owners can borrow money on their equity, the value of their home less the debt still owing, for emergencies or new investments.

Subsequently, owners can use the money made available through these loans toward renovations, increasing the value of his or her home. Renovation is sometimes necessary when there is a new member in the family and an extra room is needed. On the other hand, renters have no alternative but to move. Along with renovations, owners can paint or wallpaper without having to ask permission. Renters must, and are usually denied permission because landlords (owners) do not trust the quality of work or the taste of the renter. If landlords do agree, usually renters are not reimbursed for the supplies and work they have put in. Additionally, this increases the value of the home or property for the owners, but it does nothing for renters except perhaps make a difficult situation a little more liveable.

With the threat of having to move at the request of the landlord, renters must consider many problems that can arise from moving often. First, moving is expensive: Truck rental and connection fees for hydro, telephone, and cable add up to a great deal of money, not including the damage deposit. If renters have children, they must also think about the adjustments they will have to make. Moving from school and friends can be quite a psychological trauma for children, and they may become shy and evasive. Children who do not have this threat can feel secure, making good, long-lasting friendships.

Is owning a home better than renting? Owning allows people to renovate, invest, and feel secure in the family's well being, whereas renting means moving, having to ask permission to paint or wallpaper, and certainly causes anxiety in children. With all this taken into account, the benefits of owning far outweigh those of renting.

Definition

The definition rhetorical pattern explores what something is or what the nature of something is. Definitions ask you to look at what characteristics define something.

Examples:

> What is a friend?

> A friend is a person who trusts you to tell the truth, laughs at your jokes, and helps you build the new porch you need.

For the writer, a friend has three characteristics that distinguish friendship from non-friendship. The next paragraph is a definition of a pessimist.

> Pessimists are people with a problem. Their negative attitudes towards most things follow them everywhere they go; they see shadows instead of light, sadness instead of joy, and anger instead of laughter. Convinced that they have been born with "bad karma," they journey through life as if a permanent black cloud were over their heads. Scornful, self-pitying, sarcastic, they surround themselves with others who share their doom and gloom philosophy. Together, they revel in the misfortunes of others, natural catastrophes, and destruction wrought by humans, using these events to reinforce their belief that life is a cruel trick invented by a sadistic deity for its own amusement. As self-proclaimed experts, pessimists recount utopian visions of living, absent from the "real" world. Their cynical nature prevents them from feeling enjoyment and relaxation. Their credo is Murphy's Law—what can go wrong will go wrong—and they await the next misfortune. They have little ambition because ambition prefigures hope, and hope is for optimists—fools who live to try to find happiness in their days. Bitterness and resentment become pessimists' constant companions, and sadly, their predictions come true—loneliness follows.

What characteristics define a pessimist in this writer's view? How is a pessimist distinguished from an optimist? Are there other characteristics you want to add?

TECHNIQUES IN DEFINING   You can structure your definition using one of the following techniques:

- define by how something works.
- define by how something is put together.
- define by what distinguishes the term or idea.
- define by how something is different from something else.
- define by what something is not.
- define by where something comes from.

Examples:

- How something works: A defibrillator is a device that actually uses the body's energy in an unusual way.
- How something is put together: An ideology is a theory organized around a single common purpose.
- What distinguishes the term or idea: Space travel is unlike ground or sea transport.
- What something is not: Desire is not love.
- Where something comes from: Canadian social democracy has its roots in the prairie and in its work ethic.

When defining a quality, issue, idea, or object, be sure your definition essay has the following elements:

In the introduction:

- the term or idea you are defining
- a sentence that contains your definition
- a clear thesis with definition as a clear rhetorical mode

In the body:

- paragraphs that explore distinguishing features
- clarification, using supporting examples or anecdotes

In the conclusion:

- a renaming of your term or idea
- your summary definition

Cause and Effect

Cause and effect are relational. When you write an essay using this rhetorical mode, you must show how something influences or is influenced by something else. You consider impact, results, consequences, and outcomes in thinking through a cause and effect relationship.

Examples:

- Moderate exercise improves fitness.
  (Something influences something else.)

- Cheating on exams results in failure.
  (Something is a result of something else.)

- Good advertising brings in business.
  (Something is the consequence of something else.)

In the following paragraph, the writer explores the benefits of walking by relating walking to its positive effects.

Walking can have positive effects on the body, mind, and spirit. Beginners can start easily and feel the benefits quickly. Fitness levels can be improved by just walking around the block a few times a week. Walking helps to encourage the strengthening of bones and to reduce bone porosity, especially important to women in later life because the loss of bone density results in bone breaks. In fact, walking stimulates bone cells to build more bone. Walking on a regular basis can also decrease the need for some medications, and it can help people who have just had heart surgery with their recovery. Moreover, circulation is improved by walking, and pumping more blood through the body benefits energy levels, improves muscle tone, and generates a feeling of wellbeing that radiates into other aspects of a person's life. Furthermore, a powerful benefit is an increase of energy, which brings on a feeling of well-being. In a study carried out in 2003 at the University of Western Ontario, people reported that, after taking walks after supper, they felt more relaxed and happy than they did before the walk. Also, walking promotes safe and healthy weight loss which, in turn, makes walkers feel better about themselves. When people feel discouraged or overwhelmed by life, they feel their spirits lifted as they walk, and they seem to find solutions to many problems. The link between walking and improved health is clear; people simply have to take responsibility for their own fitness and get started.

What cause and effect connections does the writer make? What examples are used? Is the relation between walking and health clearly established? Is it convincing? Why or why not?

Example: Cause and Effect

The Effects of Stress on Everyday Living

Modern life has made people more anxious and rushed. Getting to work on time or finishing a paper can leave a person frustrated. Stress, the adjustment period to any change in life, physically, mentally, or spiritually, varies from day to day. If too many changes occur, and there is not enough time to absorb these alterations, a person will suffer from chronic stress. Stress will eventually affect family life, work capabilities, and health.

When parents are pressured to get a job done, whether it be at school, work, or even at home, their actions affect those around them. While parents are at their busiest, the children are vying for attention, negative or positive. Caught in this vicious circle, the parents become angry and impatient, which then causes the children to become more upset and erratic. For teenagers, drugs and vandalism can become their way of coping with the lack of attention and understanding. Studies done on the reasons why teenagers became delinquent found that, in most cases, it was because of a bad family situation. Stress causes people to say things and act differently. Husbands and wives lose communication, and the home becomes a place of tensions rather than relaxation.

Because stress affects sleep, it also affects how alert and energetic people are. If individuals are tired and lack motivation, the quality of work will deteriorate. Jobs that were once completed easily now take days to finish. Fellow workers also notice changes. Where they once saw a good-natured person, they now see a tired and irritable ogre. Eventually, with the lack of contact from fellow workers, the workload seems greater and becomes a burden for the employee until he or she does not care anymore.

The relationship between stress and health has also been chronicled since the beginning of the twentieth century. Although researchers are still conducting studies on this relationship, most evidence has shown that when people are mentally worn down they are more susceptible to disease and illness. Stress can cause a loss of appetite or an increase, and the effect on the body can be hazardous. Obesity is one of the major causes of strokes. In contrast, if a person is not eating, he or she begins to lack the essential vitamins and minerals that are necessary to fight off illness. Terminally ill patients have found that exercising regularly releases stress, improves their tolerance for pain, and for some extends their lives.

Whatever the causes of stress are, be it a death in the family, a heavy workload, or a lack of money, people should find positive ways of releasing it. Taking walks, exercising, or working on a relaxing hobby are very essential and should be done every day so that stress is kept to a minimum. Learning to cope with stress will not only improve people's lives but also the lives of those around them.

Classification and Division

This rhetorical mode groups ideas. A classification pattern puts things into groups, categories, or types. A division pattern describes what parts or elements make up something. For example, you may want to discuss parenthood. If you ask: "What types of parents are there?" you would be using a classification pattern. If you ask: "What makes up a good parent?" you would be using a division type of pattern. This rhetorical mode may suit your purpose if you are trying to consider ideas in a new way, perhaps to create new classifications for things. By the same token, you may find that you are asked to consider the components of something. For example, in a literature essay you may decide to define a hero as someone who is loyal, stands up for his or her own convictions, and sacrifices for others. Then, you might consider the main character of a novel and attempt to fit him or her into your definition. This division pattern is commonly used because it asks a writer, thinker, or reader to consider what constitutes something. This is a fairly straightforward pattern to use and is effective because once your categories or parts have been decided, then most of the organization of the essay has been taken care of. Use keywords and phrases like *type*, *division*, *group*, *kind*, etc.

When using this type of pattern, be careful of grouping people into categories and then making sweeping definite statements about their characteristics. Be sure your statements about people are fair and well supported.

Example: Classification and Division

Three Kinds of Drivers

Since cars were invented, western society deals with the problems and harm stemming from a variety of driving habits. Most drivers seem unaware of the potentially damaging power of the ordinary automobile. Others drive by the rules. Three types of drivers—the reckless, who is a danger; the inconsistent, who is a menace; and the circumspect, who is an exemplar of safe driving—dominate Canadian roadways.

The first type, the reckless driver, causes harm. Since most drivers in this category are male and 18–35 years of age, according to accident data, this type of driver will be referred to as "he." Largely, he does not obey posted signs and speed limits. He is caught speeding more than drivers in any other age group. He speeds while ignoring road conditions and drives according to how he feels. Secondly, this driver respects neither drivers nor pedestrians. He is seldom aware of pedestrian crosswalks or walkers, bikers, or joggers on the road. According to a 2004 Alberta Motor Association report, pedestrian deaths in crosswalks is on the rise. The ICBC (Insurance Corporation of British Columbia) also confirms this evidence in a 2003 study of fatal accidents. Property is also damaged by this driver. Some estimates claim insurance rates increase by 10 percent a year due to damage to vehicles and real property. The reckless driver causes the most harm, but another type is also dangerous.

The inconsistent driver is unpredictable. Driving habits change, depending on the driver's stress levels. Most of the time, this person obeys the road signs and the speed limits, but sometimes, he or she will take undue chances. He or she may run an amber light because he or she is late. This driver may carelessly ignore speed limits because of inattention. The inconsistent driver may suddenly change lanes without giving other drivers proper signals. He or she may weave all over the lane as the individual fumbles with a coffee cup, a cigarette, or the stereo system. This driver may like to socialize as he or she is driving down the road, paying more attention to the conversation than the road conditions. Moreover, this driving type is totally distractible. If there is a scene alongside the road, this driver will "rubberneck" in order to get a glimpse, completely unaware that by doing so, he or she has slowed traffic or made the driver behind come to a screeching halt. This driver does not intend to drive recklessly; he or she is simply unmindful, in contrast to the third type of driver.

The circumspect driver is the most reliable and is generally accident-free. This driver obeys signs, attends to speed limits, and is attentive of the road conditions. He or she drives defensively, taking in the "big picture" on the road, including construction zone speed limits, school zones, dangerous drivers in other lanes, black ice, detours, and other roadway hazards. This driver respects the road rights of others and pays close attention to pedestrians. He or she drives for safety: In rush hour traffic, this is the driver who will allow another driver to access a lane or make a lane change. He or she also respects the need to give opportunities to commercial drivers like bus or cab drivers, or truckers who drive as their livelihood. Because the circumspect driver is so expert, he or she rarely gets into collisions or causes harm on the road.

These three types of drivers are on Canadian roadways night and day. Two types create problems and harm, while the last makes driving pleasant and safe. All in all, some drivers are uneducated as to the potential damage of careless driving, and as NRW news reports, 72 percent of people killed on the roads were killed by reckless, ruthless drivers. Each driver on the road chooses the type of driver to be. With more consideration and thought, every driver could become the circumspect one.

Using a Blended Approach

Generally speaking, you will find that writers use a combination of rhetorical modes when they write, although one mode may dominate. Different modes are better suited to different purposes, so it is not unusual to see body paragraphs in different modes.

Sometimes your topic requires this flexibility. It will depend on your purpose, your audience, and your tone to some extent. For example, if your audience is a group who might require further explanation, then you may decide to define some key ideas in your first body paragraph. In the second and third body paragraphs, you might decide to compare and contrast your definitions to other popular ones, considering what is different and what is the same about them. In the paragraphs following, you might decide to discuss the impact of certain ways of representing something through the definitions—a cause and effect rhetorical mode.

Sometimes you will be assigned one particular mode to work with, but in many other writing situations, you will decide the design of your paper. A history course, for instance, may have three or four written assignments in it. Your professor or instructor will be interested in how you make your ideas relate. You may choose cause and effect, classification, and process analysis as tools to use to organize and design one paper. You may choose another set for another paper, depending on your purpose. If you wish to explore how ideas contrast in two different periods of Canadian social history—ideas of marriage, for example—then you will use this tool mainly, but you may also want to bring in definitions of marriage as part of your paper's discussion. You may also want to divide the idea of marriage into the component parts that have traditionally comprised it. Therefore, as a matter of critical thinking and writing, you will choose the appropriate rhetorical modes and thinking tools to develop your topic and to suit your specific purpose in writing.

The following article comes from a popular Canadian magazine. The writer uses a blended approach in the organization of the piece. Read the article, paying attention to the rhetorical modes Jennifer Quist uses. Since the piece is written for a magazine, you will notice some differences in paragraphing style between this article and academic writing. For example, the last part of the article is a single sentence only. In academic writing, you must use complete paragraphs in all sections of your paper.

Example: Blended Approach

It's All in the Bag

by Jennifer Quist

Jennifer Quist, her husband, and three young sons live in Fort McMurray, Alta., where she writes a weekly newspaper column.

It looks like a shrunken, leather Noah's ark with a long shoulder strap sewn onto its ends. It can still be found slumped on the third step up to the second floor of my parents' house. Inside, it's crammed with credit cards, hand lotions, tissues, gum, makeup, half a dozen pens (some that actually work), a cellophane rain hat from decades past, and a cellular phone from the cutting edge of technology. It's always been an institution of motherhood in our family—the Big Purse.

My mother isn't a cruel woman, but she is merciless when it comes to the primacy of the Purse. She has forced her own children to fetch it for her, sit crowded in shopping carts with it, and feel it tossed heavily onto our feet in the front seat of her car. She has even made us carry it in public. The loss-prevention sentinels that "greet" shoppers at discount stores bristle with even greater suspicion than usual when a teenager skulks sheepishly through the automatic doors with a behemoth handbag half-tucked under her jacket. I could almost hear the surveillance cameras zooming in to see that the bulging purse stayed shut. It was with us everywhere—the Big Purse.

It was one of those mothering institutions that I dreaded as a young girl, like varicose veins and zippered housecoats. In my younger days, as I peered at it over the tops of my sociology textbooks, the Big Purse looked exactly like a shackle of male oppression. It slouched on the stairs embodying the injustices of a society where women must be weighed down by huge, ugly sacs in order to maintain social order. In those early days, I assured myself that it must be possible for me to someday have a family of my own and at the same time resist the powerful gravity of the Big Purse.

It was also in the midst of my liberal feminist education that I decided that male power in modern society has a major seat that has been overlooked in all the excitement over pay equity and patrilineal nomenclature: the unfair allocation of pockets between the sexes.

Even in an age that has seen practical fashion movements like "cargo" clothing, there are still times when women are expected to dress in clothes that are completely devoid of pockets. This is especially true when women need to dress in formal wear or maternity clothing. Women are consistently deprived of pockets in the clothes that are designed and merchandised for us. Maybe someone is afraid that a pregnant woman with pockets would be too socially powerful. After all, a fruitful womb is the ultimate pocket known to humankind.

Regardless, most women, pregnant or not, find themselves often relying on the charity of the many-pocketed opposite sex to carry our car keys and bank cards. Men's clothing is slathered in pockets. While women teeter around dress-up affairs juggling ridiculous, shiny clutch purses and glorified wallets on strings, men tuck what they need into the nine pockets sewn into most of their suits.

Growing up is full of surprises. As my life unfolded, it turned out that things aren't quite as unfair as I had once thought. I didn't find this out all at once. It crept up on me little by little as I started having my own children. It seems that with every new phase my kids pass through, I find myself back in the accessories sections of cheap department stores rifling through tables full of cavernous, discount purses. Every time I visit the sales racks I come away with a bigger purse than the I one I brought in with me.

Now it sits in a corner of my bedroom—my very own Big Purse. It holds water bottles, baby wipes, diapers of two different sizes, Aspirin, toddler-bribing treats, half a dollar in pennies, and even something my own mother was never neurotic enough to carry herself: a coupon file.

I admit that I was wrong about the Big Purse. With my Big Purse at my side I'm almost completely self-sufficient. I can blow my nose whenever I want to because I always have a tissue. I'm the only one at noisy amusement parks with access to Aspirin. And when the baby spits up I'm the heroine, with a perpetual stash of baby wipes within arms' reach.

The Big Purse is probably not a symptom of male oppression. Instead, it might just be part of the cure for it. In the lives of women like myself and my mother, the Big Purse makes it possible for us to be independent, adaptable, in control and functional in a world that is more focussed on meeting the needs of the many-pocketed. The Big Purse doesn't embody the whimper of a defeated sex but the war cry of a resourceful gender with a workable alternative to simply mimicking its oppressors.

I lug my Big Purse with pride. It doesn't weigh me down. It helps to set me free.

Source: Jennifer Quist, "It's All in the Bag," Maclean's *1 Apr. 2002: 12. By permission of Jennifer Quist.*

Assignment: In-class Writing

Your instructor will ask you to write a short (500–600 word) essay in class, using one of the rhetorical modes or a blended approach. The instructor may select two of the readings from the readings chapter, have you read the selections in class, and then have the class develop topics. You will choose one of the topics and write your essay during class time, using about 40–45 minutes. You will have to write quickly. Make a sketch outline. Write for 30 minutes. Edit for 15 minutes. Be prepared to share your writing with the rest of the class.

Assignment: Writing an Essay

Write an essay of about 700 words on one of the following topics. Double space your writing. Use the guidelines for the first page based on MLA style documentation. (See the information on first-page set-up in Chapter 12.) If your instructor wants you to use APA style, you will also find the guidelines for setting up the first page in Chapter 12.

Topics:

- cheap recreation
- responsibilities of parenthood

- what it means to be a Canadian
- philosophy for kids
- differences between charities and corporations
- how to make a time machine
- drivers' habits
- remodelling your home
- fashion disasters
- family dinners
- the best pets
- weekend projects
- athletics and competition

Review Test

1. What is a rhetorical mode in writing?

_____

_____

_____

_____

2. What is a classification mode?

_____

_____

_____

_____

3. What is a process analysis mode?

_____

_____

_____

_____

4. What is a blended approach?

_____

_____

_____

_____

5. What is the purpose of rhetorical modes in writing?

_____

_____

_____

_____

Bonus Exercise: *Avoiding Double Negatives*

Using double negatives is placing two negative words or phrases together. This phrasing is considered incorrect. Double negatives are confusing because it is not clear if the writer wants the sentence to be positive by having one negative cancelling out the other or if the writer wants to be emphatic. The Brian's Errors website (http://www.wsu.edu/~brians/errors/double.html) provides a fun example of a double negative: "Douglas Adams' description of a machine dispensing 'a substance almost, but not quite, entirely unlike tea'."

In any case, avoid writing in double negatives.

Examples:

Error: Rochelle does<u>n't</u> have <u>none</u>. (negative + negative)

Correction: Rochelle does<u>n't</u> have <u>any.</u> (negative + positive)

Correct each of the following by eliminating the double negatives.

1. Nick doesn't want nothing for lunch.

_____

_____

2. I can't share my pizza with you because I don't have hardly any.

_____

_____

3. The dog couldn't scarcely walk after the accident.

_____

_____

4. Mr. Mueller, the new manager, has not been here barely a year.

_____

_____

5. The shopper could not find nowhere to buy new shoes.

_____

_____

CHECKOUT

Here are some of the ideas you will take away with you after you have completed the chapter:

1. Rhetorical modes shape ideas by arranging them into patterns.

2. Expository writing informs readers.

3. Key phrases help the reader follow the passage of time throughout your essay.

4. There must be some angle of interest in the thesis statement; otherwise, the reader could simply look up the information in a reference book.

5. A thesis statement tries to convince.

chapter 7

Critical Skills: Summarizing and Paraphrasing

Chapter Objectives

What will you have learned when you have completed this chapter?

You will be able to

1. recognize and understand what a summary is.

2. identify summary purposes.

3. write a paragraph summary.

4. distinguish what plagiarism is.

Introduction

The completion of your assignments in college or university will be shaped by the reading, interpretation, and discussion you do based on the work of thinkers in your field. Most courses will require you to do research for your academic papers. You can involve original material in your papers in one of three ways: you can directly quote the material (direct quotation); you can paraphrase the material (indirect quotation); or you can summarize the central ideas of the material (indirect quotation). In all three instances, you must name the author of the ideas (cite your sources). This chapter will introduce you to some of the ideas and techniques of summarizing and paraphrasing.

Self-Test

Without reading the chapter, try the following self-test to check out your understanding of summarizing and paraphrasing. Check your answers with the Answer Key.

1. In your own words, describe what a summary is.

   _____

   _____

2. In your own words, describe what a paraphrase is.

   _____

   _____

3. What is the difference between a paraphrase and a summary?

   _____

   _____

4. What are the purposes of a summary? Name two.

   _____

   _____

5. What is plagiarism?

   _____

   _____

6. What is active reading?

   _____

   _____

7. Name two goals of critical reading.

   _____

   _____

8. Write a one-sentence summary for the following. Your sentence should be no more than 20% of the original or 22 words in length.

   _____

   _____

Throughout history, people have always harboured the desire to visit distant regions or foreign lands. From ancient times through to the Middle Ages, travel by foot and by beast of burden were the predominant modes of transport, although harnessing the power of the wind allowed sailing craft to explore the seas and oceans within a limited range. The invention of the compass freed mariners to open up navigation routes, leading to astonishing voyages of discovery. Commerce and empire were the primary forces propelling small sailing vessels over the horizon and into the unknown. "Here be dragons," noted early cartographers in the margins of their crude maps of vast seas and mysterious faraway lands. (word count 113)

Source: David J. Mitchell, All Aboard! The Canadian Rockies by Train (Vancouver/Toronto: Douglas & McIntyre, 1995) 8.

9. Write a paraphrase of the passage provided in question 8.

_____

_____

_____

_____

_____

_____

_____

_____

_____

Developing Critical Reading Skills

To read critically means to be involved actively with what you read. As a reader, you are thinking about not only what a writer says but also how a writer says it. As a critical reader, you think beyond the facts by trying to interpret them.

In several sections of *Spotlight on Critical Skills in Essay Writing*, you will find discussion and practice that relate to critical reading. The chapters "Evaluating" and "Persuading" (Chapters 8 and 9) provide more information and opportunity to practise the elements of critical reading and thinking.

Goals of Critical Reading

As a critical reader, you want to engage in a lively way with what you read. Following are some of the main goals of critical reading. You may have others you wish to add to the list; however, the six given below will act as strong guidelines and will help you to develop your criticality as a reader.

1. Thinking actively about what you are reading.
2. Reflecting on what you are reading.

3. Recognizing the elements of the writer's argument.
4. Making judgments about the writer's argument.
5. Evaluating the strengths and weaknesses of the writer's argument or ideas.
6. Detecting the writer's bias.

Active vs. Passive Reading

Active reading means you are engaged and interested in the text you are reading; passive reading means you are simply going through the mechanical aspects of reading—moving your eyes across lines of text and turning pages. To read actively is important because sometimes you can fool yourself into thinking you comprehend something you are reading when you actually do not. Active reading takes practice.

Tips

- Read with a pencil. Take notes, make notations in the margins, draw diagrams, make single- or two-sentence summaries, write key phrases or terms in the margins.
- Highlight cautiously. Sometimes over-highlighting ends up being the colouring of pages rather than the reading of them. If you do like to highlight, restrict how much you highlight on a page. For example, decide to highlight only the important features of the writer's argument or thesis, not examples, data, or other facts. After you have completed the highlighting of a page, look away and write a summary of a few sentences.
- As you read, write questions in the margins or in your notebook.
- Pay attention to how ideas are organized in the text. Does the writer compare or contrast? Does the writer discuss the most important ideas first or last? Does the writer provide clear proof as support for his or her claims?
- Pay attention to the writer's style. What is the writer's tone? What is the writer's diction like? To whom is the writer speaking, do you think?

Strategies for Critical Reading

Following you will find some strategies to use and practise as you do your academic reading.

Tips

1. Read the material more than once. The first time you read something, you may be simply getting the gist of the material (gaining a general understanding), but each time you read the same material, you will have a different purpose for doing so. Do not expect to pick up everything you will need from a single reading; that is somewhat like thinking you can pack everything you will ever

need into a single suitcase. Different trips require different things, and similarly, reading for a variety of purposes produces diverse results.

2. Diagram or outline the writer's argument, particularly if the writing is difficult or dense with detail and explanation.

3. Use active questioning. Think of several questions about the text prior to reading it. As you read, use these questions to focus your attention. Some examples of questions you can use might centre on the writer's evidence, the kinds of reasoning the writer uses, or the writer's ideas compared to another's.

4. Evaluate as you read. In your second or third reading, analyze and evaluate the writer's ideas. You might consider the strengths and weaknesses of a writer's arguments, for example, or you might concentrate on the conclusions the writer draws. Your evaluation will depend on your purpose in reading, too.

Summary and Paraphrase

According to experts like Dr. Mike Rose, a celebrated professor from UCLA, one of the most needed skills you will require as a student at college or university is the capability to summarize and to paraphrase accurately. Despite the fact that your reading workload will be substantial, you must still have a working understanding of the material in order to complete your projects and various assignments.

To summarize means to sum up the central ideas in a concise way. Summaries are useful for a number of reasons. First, they enable you to determine whether you have a general understanding of something. You do not need to have detailed knowledge about everything you read. At times, your instructors will want you to have a general grasp of a theory, a textbook chapter, or a journal article. Understanding and remembering the smallest details will not be very important. For example, if you were studying educational philosophy at a first-year level, you would be expected to be acquainted with the theories of John Dewey or Paulo Freire, but you would not be expected to be aware of every detail of their thinking.

Paraphrasing, like summarizing, is putting something you have read or heard into your own words; however, when you paraphrase, you wish to stay as close as possible to the source's meaning. In other words, a paraphrase captures the essential meaning of something while a summary encapsulates the central idea or ideas. Paraphrases are longer than summaries. Both paraphrases and summaries should balance the ideas as they are represented in the original. In summarizing or paraphrasing, you should strive to represent all ideas fairly.

Therefore, many of your academic tasks will rely on being able to distinguish significant ideas or main ideas from less important, minor, or supporting details.

main ideas	**most important**
↓	↓
minor details	less important
↓	↓
sub-details	of least importance

Characteristics of Summaries and Paraphrases

Summaries
- sums up the central idea(s)
- brief (about 20% of the original)
- given in your own words

Paraphrases
- sums up the meaning of a source
- longer (often roughly the same length as the source)
- given in your own words

Examples:

The Original

Pictures can help us organize our ideas, and a picture of a writer can help us organize our ideas about the writer. The tight-drawn line of T. S. Eliot's mouth, the broad bare chest of Ernest Hemingway, the Druid-in-tweeds look of Robertson Davies—all these are with you in your imagination as you read. Is this a face we can take into our reading of Shakespeare? In particular, how does it relate to what we know of the man and his work in 1603? I stress 1603 because while the Droeshout portrait in the Folio is Shakespeare in black and white, dead and collected, setting his stamp on a posthumous anthology of his work, the Sanders portrait is Shakespeare alive, in colour, in mid-career. The Droeshout face is for book buyers; the Sanders face is the one you might have encountered if you were hanging around the Globe Theatre. (148 words)

Source: Alexander Leggatt, "The Man Who Will Not Meet Your Eyes," Shakespeare's Face, *ed. Stephanie Nolen (Toronto: Alfred A. Knopf Canada, 2002) 281.*

A Summary

We imagine a writer from his or her picture. The new colour portrait of Shakespeare fits his vibrant image more than the former black and white one. (27 words)

A Paraphrase

Since pictures can be organizational tools, a writer's portrait can assist us in thinking about a writer by helping us construct notions about him or her. We imagine the look of T. S. Eliot, Ernest Hemingway, or Robertson Davies from their photos as we read their work. Is the new portrait of Shakespeare in 1603 more fitting with what we know about him? While the earlier Droeshout black and white portrait seems to have marked the image and work of Shakespeare for all time, the new colour Sanders portrait seems more in keeping with the lively figure we conjure up from Shakespeare's work. One image seems lifeless, while the other represents someone who was very much alive. (word count: 117—79% of the original word count)

Goals of Summaries and Paraphrases

Summaries and paraphrases have similar purposes.

1. To gain a general understanding of what you read or hear.
2. To condense others' ideas accurately and effectively using your own words.
3. To bolster reading comprehension throughout college or university.
4. To prepare for research writing and other research projects.
5. To demonstrate understanding of material to your professor or instructor.

Exercise 1:   *One-sentence Summaries*

Work in a group of three. Together, write a single-sentence summary for each of the following short pieces. Use your own words. Your one-sentence summaries should be no longer than 20% of the length of the source. Be prepared to share your answers with the class.

Passage 1:

Treasured by Chinese carvers for 5,000 years, the stone was created between 50 and 185 million years ago, when two massive tectonic plates smashed together and buckled upward to create the Cordilleran mountain region that stretches from the Yukon to Mexico. In rare cases, this collision drove serpentine, rich in iron and magnesium, into igneous rock like granite. At the contact zone, the pressure and heat transformed the soft serpentine into hard nephrite jade. These surface deposits are found as boulders, some weighing many tonnes, and as outcrops. (word count: 88)

Source: Chris Tenove, "Romancing the Stone," Canadian Geographic *Jul./Aug. 2005: 44.*

Passage 2:

One of the most striking—and unsettling—experiences I've ever had is to travel by car to a place I've never visited before, then travel back along the same route. The trip out always seems to take longer than the trip back—not just a little longer, but much, much longer. I vividly remember travelling by car a few summers ago to a town in Eastern Ontario that I had never been to before, expecting that each twist and turn of the lakeside road I was following would be the one to finally reveal my destination, hoping that the crest of every hill should provide a glimpse of a church steeple, yet I drove and drove and drove with nothing but farmers' fields on one side and docks and beaches on the other. By contrast, the trip back the next day was a very different story, a brisk little drive completely free of tension, insecurity, and surprise. (word count: 157)

Source: Jay Ingram, "The Tourist Illusion," The Velocity of Honey and More Science of Everyday Life *(Toronto: Viking Canada, 2003) 79. Copyright © 2004 Jay Ingram. Reprinted by permission of Penguin Group (Canada), a Division of Pearson Penguin Canada, Inc.*

Passage 3:

Virtually all fruits and vegetables, from apples to zucchini, have become substantially inferior nutritionally. Many vegetables and fruits have lost nearly all of their iron, necessary for healthy blood. The most depleted nutrients were found to be Vitamin A, down an average of 68 percent; iron, down 76 percent; and calcium, with an average loss of 80 percent. (word count: 58)

Source: "Incredible shrinking nutrition," Better Nutrition *Oct. 2002: 22.*

Plagiarism

When you are preparing your notes for research papers or other written projects, you must be careful to name or cite all your sources. If you directly quote someone's words, you must say whose words they are. If you do not do so, then you are plagiarizing or claiming someone else's words and ideas for your own. Plagiarism is cheating. Colleges and universities have policies, often called "academic dishonesty," addressing plagiarism.

With the rise in the use of the Internet, illegal use of someone else's material and breach of copyright are commonplace. Many people believe it is quite acceptable to "borrow" someone else's work, to cut and paste it into their own papers from a web page, and claim it as their own because "everyone else is doing it." However, plagiarism is wrong, and the academic administration of your college or university will treat plagiarism as a serious offence: Some post-secondary institutes fail students caught plagiarizing; others go as far as deregistering or expelling these students. Check your university's or college's website for its policy on plagiarism. Look for its definitions and penalties.

Generally speaking, here is what plagiarism includes:

1. Copying someone's words or ideas without crediting the source.
2. Paraphrasing someone else's words or ideas without crediting the source.
3. Summarizing someone else's words or ideas without crediting the source.
4. Having someone else write, heavily edit, or completely revise a paper you claim to be your own.
5. Manipulating information so as to make it appear it is a result of your own research and thought—"fudging the results."

Sometimes students may plagiarize without realizing they have done so. They may forget to acknowledge the writer, or they may believe the information is common knowledge, and therefore, sources do not need to be cited. Some students who are new to academic research may also believe that copying someone's words or ideas is a form of flattery—they may be copying because they admire a writer or thinker. However, claiming ignorance or innocence when it comes to plagiarism will not work. Your college or university administration is interested in upholding academic standards and applying codes of ethics in regard to the research done within its purview.

You do not need to cite or acknowledge common knowledge or information in the common domain in your research papers, but at times, you may have difficulty knowing whether something is in the common domain or not. Common knowledge means knowledge that is widely accessible to the public; this information could be found in several places and is not cited. For example, the population of the Atlantic provinces of Canada is in the public domain—you could find this information in different places without its being documented. However, if you wanted to know whether the population of Newfoundland and Labrador has been impacted by employment issues, then you might find that information only in one source. In that case, you would have to cite the source because the ideas seem original to the author.

If you are in doubt whether to cite a source or not, check with your instructor or on-campus writing centre staff. If you are unable to do so and you are uncertain if the information is common knowledge or not, acknowledge the source.

Plagiarism or Not?

In the following section, you will see examples of what constitutes plagiarism and what is acceptable.

Example:

- *The original quotation from Lionel K. McPherson:*
  The language of guilt and innocence can be misleading since it brings to mind an unqualified contrast between being culpable or not.

- *Student writing—Sample A* It is my opinion that the language of guilt and innocence can be misleading since it brings to mind an unqualified contrast between being culpable or not.

- *Student writing—Sample B*
  I think that language connected to guilt and innocence is deceptive because it seems to make us think in terms of being culpable or not.

In sample A, the student merely copied Dr. McPherson's words but did not acknowledge or credit him. In sample B, the student has produced a partial paraphrase and partial direct quotation but does not credit the original writer. Both are examples of plagiarism, even though the writer of sample B may have thought what he or she had written was his or her own writing since it contains some paraphrasing.

Correction:

Sample A—Using MLA style citation:
According to Lionel K. McPherson, "The language of guilt and innocence can be misleading since it brings to mind an unqualified contrast between being culpable or not" (485).

Sample B—Paraphrase:
Lionel K. McPherson believes that how we talk about guilt and innocence can be confusing because it seems to make us judge in an unexamined way who is responsible and who is not.

Exercise 2:   *Eliminating Plagiarism*

Work in pairs. Read each of the quotations and then the student writing that follows. Decide if the student writing is plagiarism or not. If you uncover plagiarism, then correct it either by directly quoting, paraphrasing, or summarizing.

1. *Original source:*

   According to the Statistics Canada Aboriginal Peoples Survey 2001, the Manitoba First Nations population is 107,146, which is approximately 10% of Manitoba's total population with 47% of First Nations people living on reserve. The remaining 53% live in rural communities, often close to their reserve communities, or in urban centres. The median age of Manitoba First Nations people is 22.8 years, while that of the non-Aboriginal population is 38.5 years. Thus, First Nations planning for future employment and services must consider that this youthful population 'bulge' is a decade behind the mainstream population. While mainstream society is concerned with preparing for the retiring baby boomers' needs, including housing for 'empty nesters' and seniors homes, First Nations are planning for more schools and family housing.

Source: Melanie MacKinnon, RN (Grand Rapids Cree Nation), "A First Nations Voice in the Present Creates Healing in the Future," Canadian Journal of Public Health Jan/Feb 2005: S14.

Student writing:

Fifty-three percent of Aboriginal people living in Manitoba live off reserve with the median age of 22.8 years, in contrast to the non-Aboriginal population of 38.5 years, and therefore planning for First Nations, concerned with employment and housing for youth and families, is about 10 years behind the mainstream population which is now preparing for the baby boomers who will soon be retiring and leaving their family homes.

2. *Original quotation:*

"The nation is bound together by its creative artists," Berton wrote in the *Globe and Mail* in 1999, "and not by parallel lines of rusting steel."

Source: Pierre Berton, Canadian CBC News Online, 30 Nov. 2004 http://www.cbc.ca.

Student writing:

I think that Canada is held together by its artistic creativity.

3. *Original source*:

Youth homelessness is an understudied area in the Canadian context. Estimates on the enumeration of homeless youth vary depending on the criteria used. It has been estimated that there are about 150,000 runaways in Canada, while within the nation's biggest city, Toronto, the estimates of street youth vary greatly, from 5,000 by a Coalition of Youth Work Professionals to 12,000 by the Evergreen Drop-in Centre.

Source: Kelly N. Cameron, Yvonne Racine, David R. Offord, and John Cairney, "Youth at Risk of Homelessness in an Affluent Toronto Suburb," Canadian Journal of Public Health Sept.–Oct. 2004: CBCA Reference 352.

Student writing:

In my opinion, homelessness and youth have not been studied enough. For example, in the Toronto area, between 5,000 and 12,000 kids are said to be homeless, and we're just not doing much about it.

Exercise 3:   Deciding the Purposes of Writing a Summary

Different reasons a student might have for writing a summary include these:

- To use as a study tool.
- To make research information more accessible.
- To understand a writer's argument.
- To show my professor or instructor I understand the material.
- To deepen my own comprehension.
- To provide a tool for someone else to get the information quickly.

Below are some possible summary assignments you might receive at university or college. Work in pairs: Use the list of purposes above and decide the purpose or purposes of each assignment. Be prepared to share your answers.

Assignment 1: In an anthropology class, you visit a field site. You are to provide a summary of your visit. What is the purpose of this summary?

Assignment 2: Your business instructor asks you to summarize two leadership theories given in two different articles. What is the purpose of this summary?

Assignment 3: Professor Megaphone, who teaches music theory, asks you to read the first three chapters of a textbook for next week's class. The professor asks you to provide a summary of 500 words on the chapters. What is the purpose of this summary?

Assignment 4: Your philosophy instructor asks you to critique the arguments found in several articles about ethics in professional life. What is the purpose of this summary?

Assignment 5: You are given a group assignment called Roles of First Nations Women in Early Canadian Political Life to complete in your Canadian history course. You must work collaboratively with two other students. Each of you is responsible for reading and summarizing three different articles as a foundation for your project. What is the purpose of this summary?

Exercise 4:   *Paraphrasing Quotations*

Work in a small group. Together, read the quotations and construct a paraphrase for each one. Write your paraphrase on the chart paper your instructor or professor provides or on the classroom whiteboard.

1. The die is cast in Canada: there are two ethnic and linguistic groups; each is too strong and too deeply rooted in the past, too firmly bound to a mother culture, to be able to swamp the other. But if the two will collaborate inside of a truly pluralist state, Canada could become a privileged place where the federalist form of government, which is the government of tomorrow's world, will be perfected.

   Source: Pierre Elliott Trudeau, Library and Archives Canada website www.collectionscanada.ca.

2. Metrical and rhymed poetry also has the huge advantage of being mnemonic. Listen to any child delight in repeating nursery rhymes; there's an intrinsic pleasure in similar sounds, in regular rhythms. The rhythmical movement of metre connects us with the rhythmical patterns we live by: breathing, pulse, walking; sleeping and waking; day and night; the seasons, etc.

   Source: Christopher Wiseman, "Opposing the Dark Side: An Interview with Christopher Wiseman," Interviewer Carmine Starnino, Books in Canada March 2005: 32.

3. There's a financial incentive to publishing a book that I haven't overlooked. But also your lifespan is always in doubt, and a writer's lifespan in particular, so take advantage of the situation while you can because you never know when it will end.

Source: Judith Isabella [citing Laurence Gough], "Vancouver author not yet famous in hard-boiled genre," The New Islander 16 Nov. 1997: 10.

4. I first met her in Vancouver in 1965, when her incisive criticisms disillusioned me from the fond belief that my adolescent effusions constituted poetry; I last saw her on the steps of the B.C. Legislature, old and frail but still determined, protesting against the logging of the Carmanah.

Source: Stephen Scobie [about poet Dorothy Livesay], "Livesay Lived: Local poet's career spanned Canadian literary history," Monday Magazine 23.3: 14.

5. You were bringing up something that had been worrying me for a long time. I had realized that the real establishment of the literary world did not consist of the best writers, just as the establishment of the art world did not consist of the best painters. It consisted of publishers and editors and literary columnists and opinion makers like Bill French and Ken Adachi and the bureaucrats in cultural agencies like the Canada Council, the CBC and various arts councils. I recognized there was a difference between an elite, which might consist of the best writers, and an establishment. I did not particularly like either, but to belong to an elite at least implied quality, while to belong to an establishment implied only power. And I knew all about what Lord Acton and the anarchist thinkers had to say about power.

Source: George Woodcock, Essays on Canadian Writing (Toronto: Summer 1993) 134.

6. As if this heresy isn't enough, I've begun to think that perhaps the murder of the short story by Hemingway's and Carver's emulators and by schools of creative writing is the factor that has resulted in the current great swell of interest in creative non-fiction and especially in memoir writing, or as the *New Yorker* termed its featured essays, 'Personal History.' Here we once more have recovered feeling; here feeling is considered appropriate; here it is once again cherished and nourished; here there are no restrictive conventions killing the expression of emotion, or truth-telling from inside the teller of the story. Here, also, human truths are once again more important than any artificial form, structure, or convention. Here we are reading about real life again, and every reader recognizes it, and is grateful for it. Because memoir writing hasn't been a form much used by our most serious, professional writers in the last century, such writers are free to write in whatever way seems best to them, whatever way lends itself best to full and profound expression of experience.

Source: Sharon Butala, "What's the Point," University of Toronto Quarterly Fall 1999: 875.

Writing Paragraph Summaries

You may be asked to write a paragraph summary of a longer passage or article. In this case, you should apply some of the following guidelines when you prepare your summary. It is crucial that you use your own words whenever possible. Otherwise, you may be plagiarizing rather than summarizing a writer's ideas.

Guidelines for Paragraph Summary Writing

When you write summaries as paragraphs, use the following six rules, adapted from Jeanne D. Day from the University of Notre Dame.

1. Leave out unnecessary information.
2. Delete information that repeats.
3. Cluster information under larger categories whenever possible
4. Select a topic sentence. (A *topic sentence* is a sentence in a paragraph that sums up the main ideas of the paragraph.)
5. If there is no topic sentence, invent one that fits.
6. After following steps 1–5, rewrite using your own words. Sometimes special terms must be used. Avoid quoting the author's own words, unless it is completely necessary to do so.

Exercise 5:   *Writing a Summary Paragraph*

Work in pairs. Choose one of the articles below, all relating to sleep. Use the guidelines for paragraph summary writing, and together, write a paragraph summary that is approximately 20% of the original length. Be sure to start your paragraph with a topic sentence. You may use the topic sentence in the original if one is supplied; otherwise, you must invent your own. Write out your summary and be prepared to share. Include the word count at the end of your paragraph summary.

Article 1: Majority Suffer Sleep Loss, Study Says

by Siobhan McDonough

Getting a good night's sleep is hard for many adults and that often means poorer health, lower productivity on the job, more danger on the roads, and a less vibrant sex life.

"By three to four in the afternoon, I'm starting to feel brain-drained and I need that caffeine to pick me back up again," said Becky Mcerien, 50, of Philadelphia.

She gets 6.5 hours of sleep a night—slightly less than the adult average of 6.9 hours reported by the National Sleep Foundation.

Many experts say adults need a minimum of seven to nine hours of sleep a night.

A poll for the foundation, released this week, indicates that three-quarters of adults say they frequently have a sleep problem, such as waking during the night or snoring.

Most people ignore the problem and few think they actually have one. Only half of those polled were able to say they slept well on most nights.

"I get what I need to function," said Guillermo Sardina, 55, of Hamilton, N.J., who averages six or seven hours a night. "I sleep through the night. I'm a sound sleeper. . . . I don't even remember my dreams."

One-quarter of adults say sleep problems have some impact on their daily lives.

Richard Gelula, the foundation's CEO, said there's a link between sleep and quality of life.

"People who sleep well, in general, are happier and healthier," he said. "But when sleep is poor or inadequate, people feel tired or fatigued, their social and intimate relationships suffer, work productivity is negatively affected, and they make our roads more dangerous by driving while sleepy and less alert."

Symptoms of a sleep problem include difficulty falling asleep, waking a lot during the night, waking up too early and not being able to get back to sleep, waking up feeling unrefreshed, snoring, unpleasant feelings in the legs or pauses in breathing.

It's not just how much sleep a person gets, but the quality of sleep that matters, the report said.

Some of the country's sleep habits can be attributed to an always-on-the-go society, said Chris Drake, senior scientist at the Henry Ford Hospital Sleep Center in Detroit and co-chairman of the 2005 poll task force.

"In an increasing 24-hour society, people are staying up much later," he said. "They can go to a 24-hour pharmacy or supermarket. They can do anything at any time of the night and day. That can impact on people's decisions to stay up later watching TV, doing work, being on the Internet."

Mary Cuffee, 64, of Washington, says she stays up watching TV and has a stressful job. For her, seven hours of sleep aren't enough. She says she needs at least 10.

The study found:

- Six in 10 adult motorists said they have driven while drowsy in the past year; four per cent reported that they have had an accident or near-accident because they were too tired or actually fell asleep while driving.
- Three-fourths said their partner has a sleep problem, and the most common is snoring.
- Roughly one-fourth of respondents who have partners report that their sexual relationship has been hurt because they have been too sleepy. (word count: 526)

Source: Siobhan McDonough, "Majority Suffer Sleep Loss, Study Says: Bad Night's Rest Linked to Poor Health, Dangerous Driving," Times Colonist [Victoria] 1 April 2005: C6.

Article 2: Sleep Helps Us Solve Problems, Study Shows

by Patricia Reaney

Advice to "sleep on it" could be well founded, scientists said yesterday.

After a good night's sleep, a problem that seemed insurmountable the night before can often appear more manageable, although the evidence until now has been anecdotal.

But researchers at the University of Luebeck in Germany have designed an experiment that shows a good night's sleep can improve insight and problem-solving.

"If you have some newly acquired memories in your brain, sleep acts on these memories, restructures them, so that after sleep, the insight into a problem which you could not solve before increases," said Dr. Jan Born, a neuroscientist at the university.

To test the theory, they taught volunteers two simple rules to help them convert a string of numbers into a new order. There was also a third hidden rule that could help them increase their speed in solving the problem.

The researchers, who reported their findings in the science journal *Nature*, divided the volunteers into two groups.

Half were allowed to sleep after the training while the remainder were forced to stay awake.

Born and his team noticed the group that had slept after the training were twice as likely to figure out the third rule as the other group.

"Sleep helped," Born said.

"The important thing is that you have to have a memory representation in your brain of the problem you want to solve and then sleep so it can act on the problem."

But Born admitted he and his team do not know how restructuring of memories occurs or what governs it.

Pierre Maquet and Perrine Ruby of the University of Liege in Belgium said the experimental evidence supports the anecdotal suggestions that sleep can stimulate creative thinking.

"The authors [of the study] have applied a clever test that allows them to determine exactly when insight occurs in the time-course of learning," they said in a commentary.

Although the role of sleep in human creativity will still be a mystery, the research gives people good reason to fully respect their periods of sleep, they added. (word count: 342)

Source: Patricia Reaney, "Sleep Helps Us Solve Problems, Study Shows," National Post *22 Jan. 2003: A13.*

Article 3: Don't Snooze? You Lose.

by Brad Evenson

"Type A" people who practise all night or rise too early in the morning could be hampering their brains' capacity to learn and remember.

Harvard University researchers say the brain takes advantage of sleep to refresh the mechanisms it uses to perform tasks. Even a 60-minute catnap is enough to ward off mental burnout.

However, "life's modern erosion of sleep time could shortchange your brain of some learning potential," says Matthew Walker, a professor of psychiatry at Harvard Medical School. The new findings, published in the journal *Neuron,* have implications for a broad range of tasks, from swinging a golf club to playing a Mozart sonata.

These endeavours all depend on what brain scientists call "procedural memory."

Many dancers, athletes and musicians know they perform best when they stop practising a day or two before the show or competition. But it has never been clear whether it was passage of time or sleep that caused the improvement.

The Harvard University researchers say sleep is definitely the answer. In the study, they asked 62 right-handed volunteers to type the numbers 4-1-3-2-4 with their left hand as quickly and accurately as possible for 30 seconds. After 12 practice sessions of 30 seconds, subjects had improved their speed and accuracy by 60%.

A group that stayed awake for 12 hours after the morning training session showed no improvement when re-tested.

But after a night's sleep, their performance rose by almost 19%.

A second group that trained in the evening scored a 20.5% improvement after a night's sleep.

Dr. Walker and his colleagues say sleep may enhance motor skills by synchronous nerve firings called spindles—not unlike a crowd of sports fans doing the "wave" in a football stadium. These spindles peak during stage 2, non-rapid-eye-movement sleep, which most people enjoy in the two hours before waking.

"It's specifically those two hours that we have found to be most important," he said.

So people who get only six hours of sleep may be shortchanging their brains, Dr. Walker said.

In a related study published this week, another group of Harvard sleep researchers found a nap might help performance.

Reporting in the journal *Nature Neuroscience*, Sara Mednick and Robert Stickgold showed that irritation, frustration and flagging performance on a mental task could be halted with a nap.

In the experiment, subjects were asked to report the horizontal or vertical orientation of three diagonal bars against a background of horizontal bars in the lower left corner of a computer screen. Their scores on the task worsened over the course of four daily practice sessions.

When subjects took a 30-minute nap, the burnout factor was halted and their performance stopped deteriorating. A 60-minute nap actually restored performance to fresh, morning levels.

Brain recordings of naps show they contain significant amounts of "slow save sleep" which appears to be an antidote to burnout, scientists say. (word count: 477)

Source: Brad Evenson, "Don't Snooze? You Lose," National Post *4 Jul. 2002: A1–A2.*

Exercise 6:   *Paraphrasing Exercise*

Use the same article you used in Exercise 5 and work with the same partner. Paraphrase the article. Use your own words. Write your paraphrase on a clean sheet of paper or on an overhead your instructor has supplied. You will be sharing your answer with the rest of the class. Put the word count at the end of the paraphrase.

Review Test

1. What is the difference between a summary and a paraphrase?

_____

_____

_____

2. Name three purposes of a summary.

_____

_____

_____

3. What is plagiarism?

_____

_____

_____

4. Give an illustration of plagiarism.

_____

_____

_____

5. Write a summary of no more than 27 words for the following passage:

Life stages affect how individuals and their families cope with illnesses and injuries. Lifespan developmental theory states that each individual will go through a sequence of orderly, distinct stages in life. At each stage, a person has to master some developmental tasks. Each task is a growth responsibility that appears at a certain stage of an individual or family's life, and has emerged from biological needs, cultural imperatives, and family goals. These tasks must be successfully completed in order to secure present satisfaction, social approval, and future success. Failure to do so will result in dissatisfaction, social disapproval and difficulties with later tasks and life. Because individuals and families interact, individual and family life cycles often juxtapose and intertwine with each other. Understanding life-cycle theory can help the physician to assess and intervene appropriately. (word count: 134)

Source: Vincent Poon and Ed Bader, "Life-Cycle Theory: Make Use of It in Your Practice," Patient Care [Mississauga] Mar. 2005: 62.

_____

_____

_____

_____

_____

6. Use the same passage and write a paraphrase.

_____

_____

_____

_____

_____

_____

Assignment

The purpose of this assignment is to demonstrate to your instructor that you understand the similarities and differences in two writers' views on the same topic. Both discuss the uses of the cellphone.

Steps:

1. Read each of the two articles below.

2. Write a one-paragraph summary of each article. Include the word count after each summary. Your summaries should be no longer than 20% of the source material.

3. Then write a comparison and contrast paragraph between the two articles, using your summaries as the basis of your discussion.

4. Hand in your assignment, using double-spacing between the lines and a font that is 11 or 12 point in Times New Roman or another serif font.

Your assignment should look like this:

Summary paragraph 1 of article 1 (word count)

↓

Summary paragraph 2 of article 2 (word count)

↓

Comparison and contrast paragraph of the two summaries

Article 1: Digital-cam Voyeurs Lurking at UVic

by Sarah Schmidt

Hunting season is indeed open at the University of Victoria.

An online database of revealing photos of female students secretly photographed on campus, posted under the heading "Hunting season is open," has been growing since September 2003. The administration learned about the Web site a few weeks ago when a member of the university community complained, but didn't inform students of its existence.

The most recent submission of a "victim" to the "Hunted T-bars" section of the site was posted Thursday. The pictures, taken from behind at various public areas on campus, including the campus bar, library and student centre, focus on female students' buttocks and thong underwear. The young women are usually sitting.

Visitors are asked to rate each picture and provide commentary. Comments include: "I wouldn't hesitate" and "Umm . . . brb (be right back)." The photos are being taken with either camera phones or digital cameras.

Cellphone cameras, a technological craze particularly among young people, have been banned in some campus athletic facilities and private gyms in Canada for fear people would surreptitiously snap revealing photos. Saudi Arabia's highest religious authority has barred the popular gadget outright, blaming the cellphone with a built-in camera for "spreading obscenity."

David Clode, head of student services at UVic, said the school can do nothing about the Web site because the shots of women's derrieres are being taken in public places on campus and the site can't be traced to a member of the university community.

Clode added, "This person is clearly working as though people are not aware of what he's doing, although as somebody pointed out to me, how can you not be aware that you're being revealing?"

Referring to the students being photographed, he said: "Their choice of attire is their choice. I can't imagine that you don't know what the effect is of how you dress."

Joanna Groves, chairwoman of the student union, said the administration should have informed students about a photographer or photographers trolling the campus for candid shots of female students.

"It's just a violation of someone's privacy," Groves said. "It's like taking a picture up someone's skirt in a public place. It's going to make women feel unsafe. I think it's reasonable for the administration to inform women so they can be at least on guard . . . that someone might be around them trying to take those kind of pictures."

Bill C-2, legislation to amend the Criminal Code currently before Parliament, includes the creation of "an offence of voyeurism and the distribution of voyeuristic material." The proposed law makes it an offence to "surreptitiously observe or make a visual recording of a person in circumstances that give rise to a reasonable expectation of privacy, where that is done for a sexual purpose."

Const. John Price, spokesman for the Saanich police, said because the campus pictures are snapped in public places, the proposed law would not apply.

"Although it would probably be an affront to a group of people within society, it is not a criminal act. If they were photos of women in a bathroom stall or through a bedroom window, where there is a strong expectation of privacy, then yes, it would be a criminal matter."

Legal issues aside, Ottawa-based author and media critic Shari Graydon, said the Web site is a disturbing cultural artifact. It denies women's humanity by creating images focused on particular body parts, she said.

"Although the fashion statement that combines low-riding pants and thong underwear would seem designed to attract viewer attention to the underwear that's often exposed, the images are being taken without the women's knowledge.

"The images are being captured and disseminated surreptitiously, and their use on the Web site alongside the words 'hunted victims' is particularly creepy and unfortunate," said Graydon, author of *In Your Face: The Culture of Beauty and You.*

The Web site, www.peepingthong.com, is registered to a Jeff Smith, who lists an address not far from the UVic campus as his residence. The phone number provided to the Internet provider is not in service. Smith, listed as both the administrative and technical contact for the Web site, did not respond to an e-mail request for an interview.

Source: Sarah Schmidt, "Digital-cam Voyeurs Lurking at UVic," Times Colonist *[Victoria] 4 Feb. 2005: A1, A2.*

Article 2: Cellphone Poses as Diet Conscience

by Sarah Staples

Jack Lavoie might have looked like just another annoying restaurant patron flipping out his cellphone in the middle of dinner. But like thousands of Canadians, Lavoie has been trying to lose weight, and his phone has been his "virtual" diet coach.

The musician and landscaper is one of the first health conscious technophiles to try MyFoodPhone: a Canadian-designed camera phone embedded with software that forwards pictures of its owner's meals to a registered dietician.

During testing of MyFoodPhone this winter at the Universite Laval, in Quebec City, Lavoie volunteered to upload images of everything he ate to a personal web page at www.myfoodphone.com.

Once a week for two months, he received a 90-second video clip response from "Caroline," a dietician in private practice, offering feedback on his food choices and tips for improvement.

MyFoodPhone, the brainchild of Quebec City-based NATS Inc., has been offered in New York City, New Jersey and Connecticut since February, and is set to make its Canadian debut this summer.

"It's like you get a video commentary of your week in the food world. (Caroline) would tell you, 'You're not eating enough vegetables,' or 'Don't forget to drink your water.' She'd direct you along the six or seven main food types," said Lavoie.

"You really become sensitive to what you're putting in your body."

At $150 US a month, plus the cost of the phone, the service is still cheaper and more efficient than booking weekly appointments with a dietician or fitness coach, its creators say.

With no advertising other than word-of-mouth, some 150 residents of the tri-state area have signed up to take virtual consultations from 50 dieticians.

And MyFoodPhone is only the latest of a slew of software-laden cellphones, PDAs and other web-enabled diet aids aimed at helping people take control over their weight loss as never before.

"Tele-dieting" technology and services represent an expanding slice of a weight-loss market worth more than $240 billion US globally, according to the Institute of Food Technologists.

It's an opportunity projected by Marketdata to reach $61 billion US in the United States alone by 2008.

Among newly released diet novelties is "Powerseed": a pod-shaped gadget launched in January. Powerseed acts as a sort of Pavlovian egg timer, encouraging dieters to chew their food slowly by discreetly beeping or flashing a green light every thirty seconds when it's time to take a bite.

Hundreds of diet and exercise software programs are becoming available for hand-held PDAs. They include versions of the popular Atkins, Keyoe, South Beach, and WeightWatchers diets released this winter that have been adapted for palmOne Zire, Treo and Tungsten hand-helds.

For more detailed calorie monitoring there's "Bodybugg," from Pittsburgh-based BodyMedia: a web-enabled armband resembling a heart monitor that advertises "92 per cent accuracy" in calculating the energy consumed and burned daily.

The system wirelessly uploads calorie counts to a computer progam that keeps track of weight loss, and offers menu suggestions to help dieters reach their desired weight.

A different kind of calorie counter is the breathalyser-style device called "BodyGem," by HealtheTech, which calculates a person's daily Resting Metabolic Rate, or calories burned by the body while at rest.

RMR accounts for as much as 75 per cent of bodily metabolism, meaning BodyGem can theoretically be used to estimate a person's ideal caloric intake for the day. It's a nifty concept, though pricey at $1,799 US for the starter package.

Source: Sarah Staples, "Cellphone Poses as Diet Conscience," CanWest News Service Times Colonist *26 May 2005: B4.*

Bonus Exercise: *Reported Speech*

Reported speech is sometimes called indirect speech. It means you are usually talking about words someone said in the past, either the immediate past or a long time ago. You report the words spoken in the past.

Examples:

- Lina said, "I'm leaving right after the concert." (direct quotation)
- Lina said (that) she was leaving right after the concert. (reported speech or indirect quotation. Usually "that" is left out in the construction. However, it is not incorrect to include it.)

Notice that when Lina spoke she talked about her intentions at the time in the present tense; however, when you report what she said, you will use a past tense verb.

Reported speech can be called indirect speech because the person is not saying the words directly; you are indirectly reporting them.

Notice, in the direct quotation, that the quotation marks go around the words the speaker says. If a direct quotation is broken up or interrupted by a signal statement of some sort (who has said the words), then use commas around your signal statement. Begin the rest of the quotation with opening quotation marks and end with closing quotation marks. Place your end punctuation (a period, a question mark, or an exclamation mark) inside the closing quotation marks. (MLA style works differently with direct quotations. Please review the MLA section for more information.)

Example:

"My boss expected the outcome," Sunny declared, "but I was certainly surprised!"

Notice that what Sunny said is interrupted by the signal statement. The exclamation mark stays inside the quotation marks.

Bonus Exercise: *Reported Speech*

Work in pairs. Use reported speech for each of the direct quotations in the following exercise.

1. "Be sure to check as you prepare to make a lane change," advised the driving instructor.

2. The police officer said, "I've noticed a number of people still refuse to wear their seat belts."

3. One of the students observed, "The instructor has purple hair!"

4. The caller asked, "Would you mail me one of your brochures?"

5. My sister shouted, "I'm terrified of heights!"

6. The television reporter stated, "I will be meeting with the Prime Minister on Tuesday."

7. Tama replied, "I don't want any sugar in my tea."

CHECKOUT

Here are some of the ideas you will take away with you after you have completed the chapter:

1. Paraphrases are longer than summaries.

2. Summaries and paraphrases have similar purposes.

3. A critical reader will think beyond the facts by trying to interpret them.

4. When you put research material into your essay, you must cite sources.

chapter 8

Critical Skills: Evaluating

Chapter Objectives

What will you have learned when you have completed this chapter?

You will be able to

1. practise and develop critical thinking skills.
2. evaluate source materials for your research essays.
3. endeavour to be principled in your approach to evaluating.
4. measure evaluations using a set of criteria.
5. uncover arguments based on false assumptions.
6. prepare better-quality research questions.

Introduction

Frequently people find themselves in situations in which they must make decisions or choices. Sometimes the answers are simple because they require very little thinking: what to make for lunch, what route to take to the campus, what brand of milk to buy at the store, and so on. However, sometimes decisions are tough. Selecting the best answer is not an easy task. Choices may have far-reaching impacts: what school to choose, what financial plans for the future, what person to have a personal relationship with, and so on. Although you cannot always be sure you have chosen wisely, you can prepare yourself in a number of ways to become better informed so that you can fairly judge your own thinking and actions. An important critical thinking skill is evaluating. This skill is complex and requires careful consideration and practice. Almost all of your coursework will require you to evaluate some issue or topic. Often you will be asked to write an evaluation of something or to prepare a piece of research writing, including evaluation.

Thinkers and writers can develop their abilities to analyze and evaluate; they can also train themselves to be more open-minded and fair as they think critically about important issues. To become more principled in your approach to evaluating, you must learn about and practise some evaluation skills.

Self-Test

Take about 20 minutes to complete the following self-test to check your understanding. Bring your answers to class, and be prepared to share them.

Part 1: Some Terms Used in Evaluation

Define each of the following terms from evaluation. Although some of the terms have more than one meaning, your definitions should focus on evaluation.

criteria _____

analysis _____

fact _____

feedback _____

opinion _____

argument _____

assumption _____

Part 2: Purposes of Evaluation

Write down three purposes of evaluation.

_____

_____

_____

Part 3: Types of Evaluation

Write down three common types of evaluation you know of.

_____

_____

_____

Part 4: Fact and Opinion

Read each of the following statements. Write F after every statement you think is a fact; write O after every statement you think is an opinion. Be prepared to discuss the reasons you have for making your choices.

1. Camille was an extremely nervous individual who was constantly jumping at the slightest noise. _____

2. Some of the early Russian poets concerned themselves with the hierarchy of social structures in society. _____

3. Wasting too much paper is a terrible sin. _____

4. All young people should have to take sex education classes before they graduate from high school. _____

Part 5: Checking Assumptions

Read each statement. Then write down what assumptions you think the statement makes.

1. Every child enjoys Walt Disney movies.

_____

_____

_____

2. Employment is good for the soul.

_____

_____

_____

3. A strong, friendly community is what everyone wants.

_____

_____

_____

Evaluation as a Critical Skill

Many experts believe that critical thinking is the most important of all skill sets for any individual to have in the 21st century. Critical thinking comprises various subsets, and a very important one is evaluation. Training in order to evaluate an argument, a discussion, a film, a web page, or anything else that may be significant in life will take particular focus, specific time, and some mental exertion. This critical thinking skill is an accumulation of other strategies you will use as you begin to analyze, consider assumptions, question, map arguments, and reach conclusions. Critical skill development is about making connections in new ways.

You probably associate the term "evaluation" with negative events from your earlier days in school: exams, report cards, grades, tests, and so forth. However, as a student in higher education, it is important to consider evaluation from a different perspective: a positive experience that can make you a better informed and more independent learner. Bear in mind: High-quality evaluations lead to improvement.

What Is Evaluation?

Evaluation does not simply include likes, dislikes, or preference. It is not just a matter of personal taste. Instead, evaluation is the process of determining the worth of something by collecting information and assigning values in order to make effective decisions. Because evaluation is a process, it involves steps. Not everyone follows the same steps or uses the same method in evaluation, but as a student, you will find the following steps useful in your approach to evaluation.

First, you must determine the purpose of your evaluation. The purpose of an evaluation is why you are doing it and what you hope to achieve. Are you trying to decide whether something has worked or not? Are you trying to evaluate how something compares to something else? Are you evaluating so that you can improve something? (Purposes of evaluation are outlined later in this chapter.)

Next, you should decide the type of evaluation you want to use. Will your evaluation concentrate on someone's performance? Then develop a simple set of criteria you want to employ. For example, if you are evaluating a speech, you might want to include such items as clarity of voice, the speaker's tone, his or her confidence when speaking, the organization of the speech, and the attention of the audience as criteria.

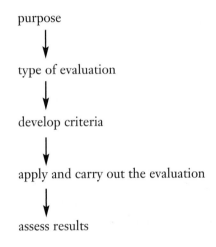

Steps for Completing an Evaluation

purpose

↓

type of evaluation

↓

develop criteria

↓

apply and carry out the evaluation

↓

assess results

Exercise 1:   *Applying the Steps for Completing an Evaluation*

Suppose you are going to buy a new computer. How would you go about deciding among all of the choices available in the marketplace and online? Use the Steps for Completing an Evaluation. Jot down your answers for each step. Be prepared to share your answers with the rest of the class.

Some Terms to Know When Evaluating

It is really helpful to familiarize yourself with new vocabulary terms as you are learning new information. This section presents you with some terms you are likely to see when you are thinking about evaluation. Of course, evaluation itself is a very complex subject or discipline, a study in itself, and this chapter is not meant to provide you with a complete list of terms. However, it is intended to give you a nodding acquaintance with some of the terms used most frequently in the process of evaluation.

1. A *fact* is a piece of information that can be verified to be true; it has been proven to be true. For instance, it is a *fact* that people need food to survive.

2. An *opinion* is a personal belief not established on proof but on a personal idea or taste. For example, "People need chocolate to survive" is an *opinion*, not a fact.

3. An *assumption* is a statement that is taken for granted as being true. For instance, "all young men love beer" is an assumption. Many arguments are based on false assumptions. As a thinker, you must uncover assumptions in arguments and test whether they are true or false, fact, or merely someone's opinion.

4. *Analysis* is the investigation of the component parts in relation to the whole of something in order to understand how it is organized. For example, if you want to use *analysis* to explore family life in the far north, you would look at what parts make up family life—kinships, roles, values, societal structures—and then you would consider each part in relation to the others.

5. *Criteria* are the standards, measures, or guidelines used when you are making an evaluation. In your college or university studies, for example, the *criteria* for passing a course may be receiving a C+ or better on all major assignments, passing two exams with C or better, and participating in two group projects. The *criteria* you set up for evaluation must be clear and workable; otherwise, the evaluation will fail.

6. *Accountability* means the obligation for responsibility or being answerable for the results of something. In a job situation, for instance, you are *accountable* to your supervisor. Your supervisor, in turn, is *accountable* to another person higher on the management ladder. *Accountability* is a tremendously important term. To illustrate, *accountability* is the basis of democracy: Democratic governments are responsible to their people.

7. *Feedback* is the response received from groups of users about products, services, ideas, policies, practices, and so forth. *Feedback* usually offers what was liked and disliked, along with suggestions for improvement. As a student, you may have been asked for *feedback* from other students on their papers, reports, or presentations.

8. An *argument* is a discussion that has a set of statements made up of premises: it ends with a conclusion supported by those premises.

9. A *valid argument* is one that has a true conclusion that flows from true premises. In this example, "I think Bailey will love this puppy because she loves dogs and always takes good care of them" is a *valid argument*. The two premises—"She loves dogs" and "always takes care of them"—are true, and the conclusion—"Bailey will love this puppy"—flows logically from them. However, an argument may contain true premises but a false conclusion; in this case, the argument is not valid. For example, "Bailey loves horses. She takes good care of them and, therefore, she will love this puppy" is not a valid argument.

10. A *sound argument* is one that has a valid argument and all true premises. The first example above is a valid and *sound argument*.

Exercise 2:   *Providing Examples*

Work in pairs. Provide examples for each of the following terms. Be prepared to share your answers.

1. a fact

   _____

   _____

2. an opinion

   _____

   _____

3. an assumption

   _____

   _____

4. a valid argument

   _____

   _____

5. a sound argument

   _____

   _____

6. an invalid argument

   _____

   _____

7. an unsound argument

   _____

   _____

Purposes of Evaluation

Why should we evaluate? We evaluate according to specific purposes. We do not evaluate everything in exactly the same way all the time. The following lists a variety of possible purposes for evaluating. Read over the list and think about the examples. Then do the exercise that follows; the list is in no particular order of importance.

Purpose 1: To Improve Something

A manufacturer may be seriously concerned that sales of one of its key products are dropping off dramatically. The manufacturer may decide to improve the product to boost sales; however, in order to know if the new product is actually better than the original, the company has to evaluate if it is really better. The company may have a number of strategies to check out the improved product with the consumer, but it knows it must evaluate, using criteria to compare the new, improved product to the original. In another example, think of some of the evaluations you have received for assignments you are asked to do in your courses. Aren't some of them based on the idea of improvement?

Purpose 2: To Make an Individual, Group, or Organization Accountable

Some individuals or organizations have heavy social responsibilities. Often they are funded publicly and must report in a responsible way to the government or to the citizenry. Democratic governments are said to be democratic because they are answerable or responsible to the people. Groups hired by government to do specific tasks are also accountable for their performance, service, products, or actions. Voting may be considered the ultimate form of evaluation of a democratic government's tenure: If people have liked the job government has done during its term, then they vote for a second term of that government. If they do not agree that government has done an effective job, then they "vote them out." Civil servants are evaluated according to the service they have given government. For example, teachers are evaluated by provincial governments according to whether they have met the evaluation criteria for effective teaching based on learning outcomes, student evaluations, supervisors' reports, and the performance of their students.

Purpose 3: To Check Progress and Assist Planning

It is sometimes difficult to know how someone or some organization is getting along with a project or task. In order to determine their progress, a supervising or managing agency will do evaluations as part of project planning. For example, if a city is funding the building of a new convention centre using tax dollars, the city has a responsibility to meet its obligations. The convention centre project may have several evaluations along the way to be sure it is running according to plan. In this way, the city is being responsible in the management of its projects and expenditures. Planning and budgeting will then be adjusted according to the results of the evaluations.

Purpose 4: To Check If an Argument Is Sound and Valid

Thinkers may be hired to evaluate whether or not an argument being presented is sound and valid. (You will learn more about soundness and validity of arguments in Chapter 9, Persuading.) An argument is sound if all its components and its conclusion are true; an argument is valid if it has been shown to be true and if the argument follows from its parts. Judges, for example, must decide if arguments presented in court are admissible according to law and to the structure of arguments provided.

Purpose 5: To Measure Outcomes or Success

Products or services may be provided, but in order to know whether they have met their objectives and are successful or not, they must be evaluated. A course or program you take at college or university is evaluated according to learning outcomes and according to whether or not students have satisfied the evaluation criteria and complete the course successfully. In some programs, student follow-up evaluations may take several years to determine if graduates have been adequately prepared in various professions. Universities and colleges want to know how successful their graduates are as doctors, lawyers, engineers, teachers, government workers, and so on.

Purpose 6: To Check How Appropriate Something Is

Industry often tries out new products in new situations. In order to determine if products are appropriate in new situations or a new product in a traditional situation, companies must evaluate. For example, a company might have a new design for a baby stroller that can be used on the beach or on rough terrain. It tests the product but then must evaluate whether consumers find the new use appropriate or not.

Purpose 7: To Maintain Standards

Professional organizations may certify if a professional's performance is up to the standards set or not. Manufacturers may also have to produce and test products that meet industry and government standards.

Purpose 8: To Make a Purchase

Consumers always want to get the "best buy" possible, so they do their own homegrown research: They investigate consumer information on products, read manufacturers' brochures, do Internet searches, talk to salespeople, and get opinions from other consumers. After they have collected all their data, they evaluate it, often by comparing and contrasting the information.

Purpose 9: To Determine the Authenticity of a Source

A critical skill in life is to be able to estimate what kind of information is being provided and if it is reliable. For example, most people use the Internet to do personal or academic research, but it is not always easy to judge if the information is accurate or if the person providing it is really the expert he or she claims to be. University and college students must pay close attention to the sources they use for their research. Bad sources lead to misinformation.

In all circumstances, effective evaluation on an important issue is not simply a case of whether someone likes it or not. Extremely useful for evaluating is having a set of criteria by which evaluation is referenced and measured.

Exercise 3:   Recognizing the Purposes of Evaluation

Work in pairs for this exercise. Read each of the scenario statements that follow. Use the purposes for evaluation outlined in the previous section as your guide, and decide which purpose for evaluation bests suits each situation. Then write the number after each statement. Be prepared to defend your selection.

1. A large engineering firm has been hired to construct a floodway system for a small prairie city. It is now one month into the project.

2. Several English students are doing an assignment together on the Canadian poet George Bowering. They have come across some copies of letters purportedly written by one of his acquaintances. The group wants to include some of the information found in the letters.

3. A new employee is being considered for a permanent position as a system information technologist.

4. Two sisters are planning to buy a used car together. They have never owned a car before and are uncertain what to look for.

5. A student lawyer is just about to take her final exams; after this, if she passes, she will be accepted into "the bar."

6. A tenant is complaining to his landlord about the condition of the small, expensive apartment he rents. He has provided the landlord with a document outlining his concerns.

7. The Board of Governors at the University of Prestige is wanting to adopt a set of policies from another university to be applied to its three new on-campus daycares.

8. The professor who teaches English 200, Advanced Composition, regularly asks students to do peer reviews of their working drafts before they hand in assignments.

9. A new program offered by the local municipality through its Continuing Studies Branch is under threat of being cut. The program called "Teenagers as Coaches" has been extremely popular. Many community members do not want to see the program deleted from Continuing Studies.

10. A young police officer, only on the job for three weeks, meets an aggressive driver whom the officer has asked to pull over. The driver claims he does not need to provide information on a form the officer has handed him.

11. The town council of a small Ontario town wants to know if the new information retrieval system it has purchased is working effectively.

12. The president of a large Canadian university is in her third year of a five-year appointment. Some faculty members claim the president is not doing a very good job. Others suggest she has been very effective.